# BEAUTIFUL STORIES
## FROM SHAKESPEARE
## FOR CHILDREN

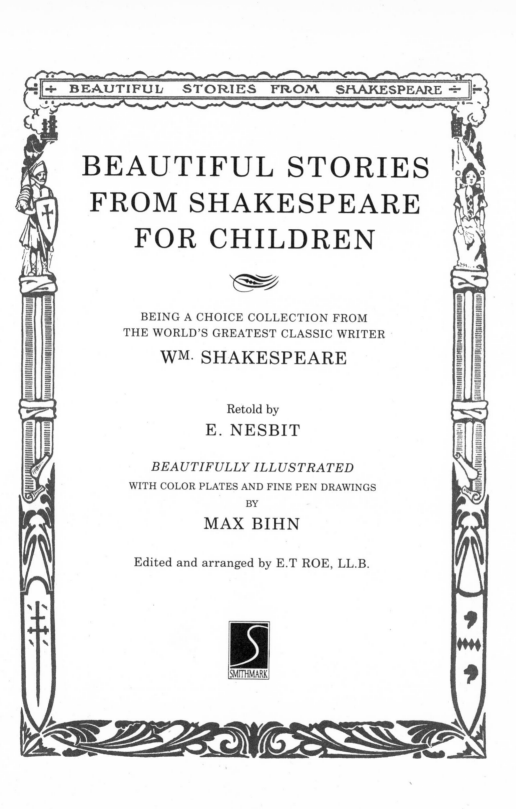

# BEAUTIFUL STORIES FROM SHAKESPEARE FOR CHILDREN

BEING A CHOICE COLLECTION FROM
THE WORLD'S GREATEST CLASSIC WRITER

## WM. SHAKESPEARE

Retold by

## E. NESBIT

*BEAUTIFULLY ILLUSTRATED*
WITH COLOR PLATES AND FINE PEN DRAWINGS
BY

## MAX BIHN

Edited and arranged by E.T ROE, LL.B.

SMITHMARK

*"It may be said of Shakespeare, that from his works may be collected a system of civil and economic prudence. He has been imitated by all succeeding writers; and it may be doubted whether from all his successors, more maxims of theoretical knowledge, or more rules of practical prudence can be collected than he alone has given to his country."*

—DR. SAMUEL JOHNSON

This edition published in 1997 by
SMITHMARK Publishers
a division of US Media Holdings, Inc.
16 East 32nd Street, New York, NY 10016

SMITHMARK books are available for bulk purchase
for sales, promotion, and premium use.
For details, write or call the manager of special sales,
SMITHMARK Publishers
16 East 32nd Street
New York, NY 10016
(212) 532-6600

Printed in the United States of America

From the private collection of Wendy D. Friedman

ISBN: 0-7651-9490-2

10  9  8  7  6  5  4  3  2  1

## PREFACE

The writings of Shakespeare have been justly termed " the richest, the purest, the fairest, that genius uninspired ever penned."

Shakespeare instructed by delighting. His plays alone (leaving mere science out of the question), contain more actual wisdom than the whole body of English learning. He is the teacher of all good — pity, generosity, true courage, love. His bright wit is cut out " into little stars." His solid masses of knowledge are meted out in morsels and proverbs, and thus distributed, there is scarcely a corner of the English-speaking world to-day which he does not illuminate, or a cottage which he does not enrich. His bounty is like the sea, which, though often unacknowledged, is everywhere felt. As his friend, Ben Jonson, wrote of him, " He was not of an age but for all time." He ever kept the highroad of human life whereon all travel. He did not pick out by-paths of feeling and sentiment. In his creations we have no moral highwaymen, sentimental thieves, interesting villains, and amiable, elegant adventuresses — no delicate entanglements of situation, in which the grossest images are presented to the mind disguised under the superficial attraction of style and sentiment. He flattered no bad passion, disguised no vice in the garb of virtue, trifled with no just and generous principle. While causing us to laugh at folly, and shudder at crime, he still preserves our love for our fellow-beings, and our reverence for ourselves.

Shakespeare was familiar with all beautiful forms and images, with all that is sweet or majestic in the simple aspects of nature, of that indestructible love of flowers and fragrance, and dews, and clear waters — and soft airs and sounds, and bright skies and woodland solitudes, and moonlight bowers, which are the material elements of poetry,— and with that fine sense of their indefinable relation to mental emotion, which is its essence and vivifying soul — and which, in the midst of his most busy and tragical scenes, falls like gleams of sunshine on rocks and ruins — contrasting with all that is rugged or repulsive, and reminding us of the existence of purer and brighter elements.

These things considered, what wonder is it that the works of Shakespeare, next to the Bible, are the most highly esteemed of all the classics of English literature. " So extensively have the characters of Shakespeare been drawn upon by artists, poets, and writers of fiction," says an American author,—" So interwoven are these characters in the great body of English literature, that to be ignorant of the plot of these dramas is often a cause of embarrassment."

But Shakespeare wrote for grown-up people, for men and women, and in words that little folks cannot understand.

Hence this volume. To reproduce the entertaining stories contained in the plays of Shakespeare, in a form so simple that children can understand and enjoy them, was the object had in view by the author of these Beautiful Stories from Shakespeare.

And that the youngest readers may not stumble in pronouncing any unfamiliar names to be met with in the stories, the editor has prepared and included in the volume a Pronouncing Vocabulary of Difficult Names. To which is added a collection of Shakespearean Quotations, classified in alphabetical order, illustrative of the wisdom and genius of the world's greatest dramatist. E. T. R.

5

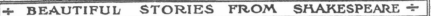

## A BRIEF LIFE OF SHAKESPEARE.

In the register of baptisms of the parish church of Strat-ford-upon-Avon, a market town in Warwickshire, England, appears, under date of April 26, 1564, the entry of the baptism of William, the son of John Shakspeare. The entry is in Latin —" Gulielmus filius Johannis Shakspeare."

The date of William Shakespeare's birth has usually been taken as three days before his baptism, but there is certainly no evidence of this fact.

The family name was variously spelled, the dramatist himself not always spelling it in the same way. While in the baptismal record the name is spelled " Shakspeare," in several authentic autographs of the dramatist it reads " Shakspere," and in the first edition of his works it is printed " Shakespeare."

Halliwell tells us, that there are not less than thirty-four ways in which the various members of the Shakespeare family wrote the name, and in the council-book of the cor-

7

poration of Stratford, where it is introduced one hundred and sixty-six times during the period that the dramatist's father was a member of the municipal body, there are fourteen different spellings. The modern "Shakespeare" is not among them.

Shakespeare's father, while an alderman at Stratford, appears to have been unable to write his name, but as at that time nine men out of ten were content to make their mark for a signature, the fact is not specially to his discredit.

The traditions and other sources of information about the occupation of Shakespeare's father differ. He is described as a butcher, a woolstapler, and a glover, and it is not impossible that he may have been all of these simultaneously or at different times, or that if he could not properly be called any one of them, the nature of his occupation was such as to make it easy to understand how the various traditions sprang up. He was a landed proprietor and cultivator of his own land even before his marriage, and he received with his wife, who was Mary Arden, daughter of a country gentleman, the estate of Asbies, 56 acres in extent. William was the third child. The two older than he were daughters, and both probably died in infancy. After him

8

was born three sons and a daughter. For ten or twelve years at least, after Shakespeare's birth his father continued to be in easy circumstances. In the year 1568 he was the high bailiff or chief magistrate of Stratford, and for many years afterwards he held the position of alderman as he had done for three years before. To the completion of his tenth year, therefore, it is natural to suppose that William Shakespeare would get the best education that Stratford could afford. The free school of the town was open to all boys, and like all the grammar-schools of that time, was under the direction of men who, as graduates of the universities, were qualified to diffuse that sound scholarship which was once the boast of England. There is no record of Shakespeare's having been at this school, but there can be no rational doubt that he was educated there. His father could not have procured for him a better education anywhere. To those who have studied Shakespeare's works without being influenced by the old traditional theory that he had received a very narrow education, they abound with evidences that he must have been solidly grounded in the learning, properly so called, was taught in the grammar schools.

There are local associations connected with Stratford

9

which could not be without their influence in the formation of young Shakespeare's mind. Within the range of such a boy's curiosity were the fine old historic towns of Warwick and Coventry, the sumptuous palace of Kenilworth, the grand monastic remains of Evesham. His own Avon abounded with spots of singular beauty, quiet hamlets, solitary woods. Nor was Stratford shut out from the general world, as many country towns are. It was a great highway, and dealers with every variety of merchandise resorted to its markets. The eyes of the poet dramatist must always have been open for observation. But nothing is known positively of Shakespeare from his birth to his marriage to Anne Hathaway in 1582, and from that date nothing but the birth of three children until we find him an actor in London about 1589.

How long acting continued to be Shakespeare's sole profession we have no means of knowing, but it is in the highest degree probable that very soon after arriving in London he began that work of adaptation by which he is known to have begun his literary career. To improve and alter older plays not up to the standard that was required at the time was a common practice even among the best dramatists

10

of the day, and Shakespeare's abilities would speedily mark him out as eminently fitted for this kind of work. When the alterations in plays originally composed by other writers became very extensive, the work of adaptation would become in reality a work of creation. And this is exactly what we have examples of in a few of Shakespeare's early works, which are known to have been founded on older plays.

It is unnecessary here to extol the published works of the world's greatest dramatist. Criticism has been exhausted upon them, and the finest minds of England, Germany, and America have devoted their powers to an elucidation of their worth.

Shakespeare died at Stratford on the 23d of April, 1616. His father had died before him, in 1602, and his mother in 1608. His wife survived him till August, 1623. His son Hamnet died in 1596 at the age of eleven years. His two daughters survived him, the eldest of whom, Susanna, had, in 1607, married a physician of Stratford, Dr. Hall. The only issue of this marriage, a daughter named Elizabeth, born in 1608, married first Thomas Nasbe, and afterwards Sir John Barnard, but left no children by either marriage.

Shakespeare's younger daughter, Judith, on the 10th of February, 1616, married a Stratford gentleman named Thomas Quincy, by whom she had three sons, all of whom died, however, without issue. There are thus no direct descendants of Shakespeare.

Shakespeare's fellow-actors, fellow-dramatists, and those who knew him in other ways, agree in expressing not only admiration of his genius, but their respect and love for the man. Ben Jonson said, "I love the man, and do honor his memory, on this side idolatry, as much as any. He was indeed honest, and of an open and free nature." He was buried on the second day after his death, on the north side of the chancel of Stratford church. Over his grave there is a flat stone with this inscription, said to have been written by himself:

Good friend for Jesus sake forbeare
To digg the dust encloasèd heare:
Blest be ye man yt spares these stones,
And curst be he yt moves my bones.

## CONTENTS

## ILLUSTRATIONS

15

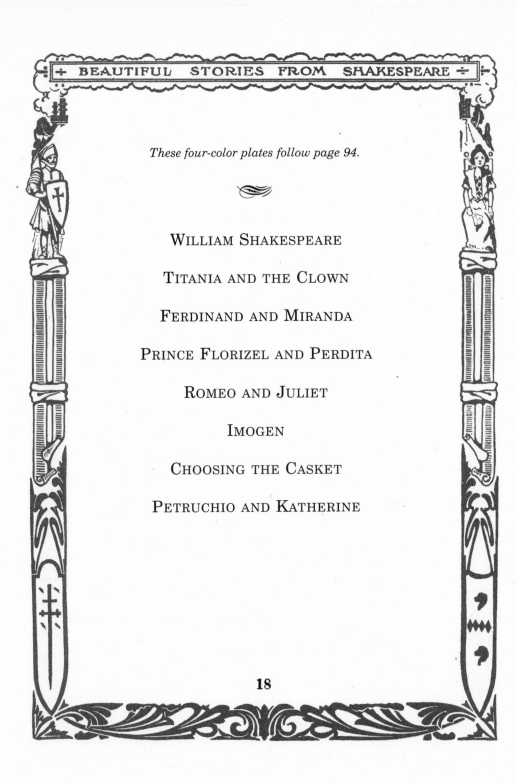

*These four-color plates follow page 94.*

## A MIDSUMMER NIGHT'S DREAM

HERMIA and Lysander were lovers; but Hermia's father wished her to marry another man, named Demetrius.

Now, in Athens, where they lived, there was a wicked law, by which any girl who refused to marry according to her father's wishes, might be put to death. Hermia's father was so angry with her for refusing to do as he wished, that he actually brought her before the Duke of Athens to ask that she might be killed, if she still refused to obey him. The Duke gave her four days to think about it, and, at the end of that time, if she still refused to marry Demetrius, she would have to die.

Lysander of course was nearly mad with grief, and the best thing to do seemed to him for Hermia to run away to his aunt's house at a place beyond the reach of that cruel law; and there he would come

19

TITANIA:
THE QUEEN OF
THE FAIRIES.

to her and marry her. But before she started, she told her friend, Helena, what she was going to do.

Helena had been Demetrius' sweetheart long before his marriage with Hermia had been thought of, and being very silly, like all jealous people, she could not see that it was not poor Hermia's fault that Demetrius wished to marry her instead of his own lady, Helena. She knew that if she told Demetrius that Hermia was

20

going, as she was, to the wood outside Athens, he would follow her, "and I can follow him, and at least I shall see him," she said to herself. So she went to him, and betrayed her friend's secret.

Now this wood where Lysander was to meet Hermia, and where the other two had decided to follow them, was full of fairies, as most woods are, if one only had the eyes to see them, and in this wood on this night were the King and Queen of the fairies, Oberon and Titania. Now fairies are very wise people, but now and then they can be quite as foolish as mortal folk. Oberon and Titania, who might have been as happy as the days were long, had thrown away all their joy in a foolish quarrel. They never met without saying disagreeable things to each other, and scolded each other so dreadfully that all their little fairy followers, for fear, would creep into acorn cups and hide them there.

So, instead of keeping one happy Court and dancing all night through in the moonlight, as is fairies' use, the King with his attendants wandered through one part of the wood, while the Queen with hers kept state in another. And the cause of all this trouble

21

was a little Indian boy whom Titania had taken to be one of her followers. Oberon wanted the child to follow him and be one of his fairy knights; but the Queen would not give him up.

On this night, in a mossy moonlit glade, the King and Queen of the fairies met.

THE QUARREL.

"Ill met by moonlight, proud Titania," said the King.

"What! jealous, Oberon?" answered the Queen. "You spoil everything with your quarreling. Come, fairies, let us leave him. I am not friends with him now."

"It rests with you to make up the quarrel," said the King.

"Give me that little Indian boy, and I will again be your humble servant and suitor."

22

"Set your mind at rest," said the Queen. "Your whole fairy kingdom buys not that boy from me. Come, fairies."

And she and her train rode off down the moonbeams.

"Well, go your ways," said Oberon. "But I ll be even with you before you leave this wood."

Then Oberon called his favorite fairy, Puck. Puck was the spirit of mischief. He used to slip into the dairies and take the cream away, and get into the churn so that the butter would not come, and turn the beer sour, and lead people out of their way on dark nights and then laugh at them, and tumble people's stools from under them when they were going to sit down, and upset their hot ale over their chins when they were going to drink.

"Now," said Oberon to this little sprite, "fetch me the flower called Love-in-idleness. The juice of that little purple flower laid on the eyes of those who sleep will make them, when they wake, to love the first thing they see. I will put some of the juice of that flower on my Titania's eyes, and when she wakes she will love the first thing she sees, were it

23

lion, bear, or wolf, or bull, or meddling monkey, or a busy ape."

While Puck was gone, Demetrius passed through the glade followed by poor Helena, and still she told him how she loved him and reminded him of all his promises, and still he told her that he did not and could not love her, and that his promises were nothing. Oberon was sorry for poor Helena, and when Puck returned with the flower, he bade him follow Demetrius and put some of the juice on his eyes, so that he might love Helena when he woke and looked on her, as much as she loved him. So Puck set off, and wandering through the wood found, not Demetrius, but Lysander, on whose eyes he put the juice; but when Lysander woke, he saw not his own Hermia, but Helena, who was walking through the wood looking for the cruel Demetrius; and directly he saw her he loved her and left his own lady, under the spell of the purple flower.

When Hermia woke she found Lysander gone, and wandered about the wood trying to find him. Puck went back and told Oberon what he had done, and Oberon soon found that he had made a mistake,

HELENA IN THE WOOD.

and set about looking for Demetrius, and having
found him, put some of the juice on his eyes. And
the first thing Demetrius saw when he woke was also

Helena. So now Demetrius and Lysander were both following her through the wood, and it was Hermia's turn to follow her lover as Helena had done before. The end of it was that Helena and Hermia began to quarrel, and Demetrius and Lysander went off to fight. Oberon was very sorry to see his kind scheme to help these lovers turn out so badly. So he said to Puck—

"These two young men are going to fight. You must overhang the night with drooping fog, and lead them so astray, that one will never find the other. When they are tired out, they will fall asleep. Then drop this other herb on Lysander's eyes. That will give him his old sight and his old love. Then each man will have the lady who loves him, and they will all think that this has been only a Midsummer Night's Dream. Then when this is done, all will be well with them."

So Puck went and did as he was told, and when the two had fallen asleep without meeting each other, Puck poured the juice on Lysander's eyes, and said:—

26

"When thou wakest,
Thou takest
True delight
In the sight
Of thy former lady's eye:
Jack shall have Jill;
Nought shall go ill."

Meanwhile Oberon found Titania asleep on a bank where grew wild thyme, oxlips, and violets, and woodbine, musk-roses and eglantine. There Titania always slept a part of the night, wrapped in the enameled skin of a snake. Oberon stooped over her and laid the juice on her eyes, saying:—

"What thou seest when thou wake,
Do it for thy true love take."

Now, it happened that when Titania woke the first thing she saw was a stupid clown, one of a party of players who had come out into the wood to rehearse their play. This clown had met with Puck, who had clapped an ass's head on his shoulders so that it looked as if it grew there. Directly Titania woke and saw this dreadful monster, she said, "What angel is this? Are you as wise as you are beautiful?"

27

"If I am wise enough to find my way out of this wood, that's enough for me," said the foolish clown.

"Do not desire to go out of the wood," said Titania. The spell of the love-juice was on her, and to her the clown seemed the most beautiful and delightful creature on all the earth. "I love you," she went on. "Come with me, and I will give you fairies to attend on you."

So she called four fairies, whose names were Peaseblossom, Cobweb, Moth, and Mustardseed.

"You must attend this gentleman," said the Queen. "Feed him with apricots and dewberries, purple grapes, green figs, and mulberries. Steal honey-bags for him from the humble-bees, and with the wings of painted butterflies fan the moonbeams from his sleeping eyes."

"I will," said one of the fairies, and all the others said, "I will."

"Now, sit down with me," said the Queen to the clown, "and let me stroke your dear cheeks, and stick musk-roses in your smooth, sleek head, and kiss your fair large ears, my gentle joy."

"Where's Peaseblossom?" asked the clown with

28

the ass's head. He did not care much about the Queen's affection, but he was very proud of having fairies to wait on him. "Ready," said Peaseblossom.

"Scratch my head, Peaseblossom," said the clown. "Where's Cobweb?" "Ready," said Cobweb.

"Kill me," said the clown, "the red bumble-bee on the top of the thistle yonder, and bring me the honey-bag. Where's Mustardseed?"

"Ready," said Mustardseed.

"Oh, I want nothing," said the clown. "Only just help Cobweb to scratch. I must go to the barber's, for methinks I am marvelous hairy about the face."

"Would you like anything to eat?" said the fairy Queen.

"I should like some good dry oats," said the clown —for his donkey's head made him desire donkey's food—"and some hay to follow."

"Shall some of my fairies fetch you new nuts from the squirrel's house?" asked the Queen.

"I'd rather have a handful or two of good dried peas," said the clown. "But please don't let any of your people disturb me; I am going to sleep."

29

Then said the Queen, "And I will wind thee in my arms."

And so when Oberon came along he found his beautiful Queen lavishing kisses and endearments on a clown with a donkey's head.

TITANIA PLACED UNDER A SPELL.

And before he released her from the enchantment, he persuaded her to give him the little Indian boy he so much desired to have. Then he took pity on her, and threw some juice of the disenchanting

30

flower on her pretty eyes; and then in a moment she saw plainly the donkey-headed clown she had been loving, and knew how foolish she had been.

Oberon took off the ass's head from the clown, and left him to finish his sleep with his own silly head lying on the thyme and violets.

Thus all was made plain and straight again. Oberon and Titania loved each other more than ever. Demetrius

TITANIA AWAKES.

thought of no one but Helena, and Helena had never had any thought of anyone but Demetrius.

As for Hermia and Lysander, they were as loving a couple as you could meet in a day's march, even through a fairy wood.

31

So the four mortal lovers went back to Athens and were married; and the fairy King and Queen live happily together in that very wood at this very day.

The TEMPEST

PROSPERO, the Duke of Milan, was a learned and studious man, who lived among his books, leaving the management of his dukedom to his brother Antonio, in whom indeed he had complete trust. But that trust was ill-rewarded, for Antonio wanted to wear the duke's crown himself, and, to gain his ends, would have killed his brother but for the love the people bore him. However, with the help of Prospero's great enemy, Alonso, King of Naples, he managed to get into his hands the dukedom with all its honor, power, and riches. For they took Prospero to sea, and when they were far away from land, forced him into a little boat with

33

no tackle, mast, or sail. In their cruelty and hatred they put his little daughter, Miranda (not yet three years old), into the boat with him, and sailed away, leaving them to their fate.

But one among the courtiers with Antonio was true to his rightful master, Prospero. To save the duke from his enemies was impossible, but much could be done to remind him of a subject's love. So this worthy lord, whose name was Gonzalo, secretly placed in the boat some fresh water, provisions, and clothes, and what Prospero valued most of all, some of his precious books.

The boat was cast on an island, and Prospero and his little one landed in safety. Now this island was enchanted, and for years had lain under the spell of a fell witch, Sycorax, who had imprisoned in the trunks of trees all the good spirits she found there. She died shortly before Prospero was cast on those shores, but the spirits, of whom Ariel was the chief, still remained in their prisons.

Prospero was a great magician, for he had devoted himself almost entirely to the study of magic during the years in which he allowed his brother to manage the affairs of Milan. By his art he set free the imprisoned spirits, yet kept them obedient to his will, and they were more truly his subjects than his people in Milan had been. For he treated them kindly as long as they did his bidding, and he exercised his power over them wisely and well. One creature alone he found it necessary to treat with harshness: this was Caliban, the son of the wicked old witch, a hideous, deformed monster, horrible to look on, and vicious and brutal in all his habits.

When Miranda was grown up into a maiden, sweet and fair to see, it chanced that Antonio and Alonso, with Sebastian, his brother, and Ferdinand, his son, were at sea together with old Gonzalo, and their ship came near Prospero's island. Prospero, knowing they were there, raised by his art a great storm, so that even the sailors on board gave themselves up for lost; and first among them all Prince Ferdinand leaped into the sea, and, as his father thought in his grief, was drowned. But Ariel brought him safe ashore; and all the rest of the crew, although they were washed overboard, were landed unhurt in different parts of the island, and the good

35

ship herself, which they all thought had been wrecked, lay at anchor in the harbor whither Ariel had brought her. Such wonders could Prospero and his spirits perform.

While yet the tempest was raging, Prospero showed his daughter the brave ship laboring in the trough of the sea, and told her that it was filled with living human beings like themselves. She, in pity of their lives, prayed him who had

PRINCE FERDINAND IN THE SEA.

raised this storm to quell it. Then her father bade her to have no fear, for he intended to save every one of them.

Then, for the first time, he told her the story of his life and hers, and that he had caused this storm to rise in order that his enemies, Antonio and Alonso, who were on board, might be delivered into his hands.

When he had made an end of his story he charmed her into sleep, for Ariel was at hand, and he had work for him to do. Ariel, who longed for his complete freedom, grumbled to be kept in drudgery, but on being threateningly reminded of all the sufferings he had undergone when Sycorax ruled in the land, and of the debt of gratitude he owed to the master who had made those sufferings to end, he ceased to complain, and promised faithfully to do whatever Prospero might command.

"Do so," said Prospero, "and in two days I will discharge thee."

Then he bade Ariel take the form of a water nymph and sent him in search of the young prince. And Ariel, invisible to Ferdinand, hovered near him, singing the while—

> " Come unto these yellow sands
>     And then take hands:
> Court'sied when you have, and kiss'd
>     (The wild waves whist),
> Foot it featly here and there;
> And, sweet sprites, the burden bear! "

And Ferdinand followed the magic singing, as the song changed to a solemn air, and the words brought grief to his heart, and tears to his eyes, for thus they ran—

" Full fathom five thy father lies;
    Of his bones are coral made.
Those are pearls that were his eyes,
    Nothing of him that doth fade,
But doth suffer a sea-change
Into something rich and strange.
Sea-nymphs hourly ring his knell.
Hark! now I hear them,— ding dong bell!"

And so singing, Ariel led the spell-bound prince into the presence of Prospero and Miranda. Then, behold! all happened as Prospero desired. For Miranda, who had never, since she could first remember, seen any human being save her father, looked on the youthful prince with reverence in her eyes, and love in her secret heart.

"I might call him," she said, "a thing divine, for nothing natural I ever saw so noble!"

And Ferdinand, beholding her beauty with wonder and delight, exclaimed—

"Most sure the goddess on whom these airs attend!"

Nor did he attempt to hide the passion which she inspired in him, for scarcely had they exchanged half a dozen sentences, before he vowed to make her his queen if she were willing. But Prospero, though secretly delighted, pretended wrath.

"You come here as a spy," he said to Ferdinand. "I will manacle your neck and feet together, and you shall feed on fresh water mussels, withered roots

PRINCE FERDINAND SEES MIRANDA.

and husk, and have sea-water to drink. Follow."

"No," said Ferdinand, and drew his sword. But on the instant Prospero charmed him so that he stood there like a statue, still as stone; and Miranda in terror prayed her father to have mercy on her lover. But he harshly refused her, and made Ferdinand follow him to his cell. There he set the Prince to

39

work, making him remove thousands of heavy logs of timber and pile them up; and Ferdinand patiently obeyed, and thought his toil all too well repaid by the sympathy of the sweet Miranda.

She in very pity would have helped him in his hard work, but he would not let her, yet he could not keep from her the secret of his love, and she, hearing it, rejoiced and promised to be his wife.

Then Prospero released him from his servitude, and glad at heart, he gave his consent to their marriage.

"Take her," he said, "she is thine own."

In the meantime, Antonio and Sebastian in another part of the island were plotting the murder of Alonso, the King of Naples, for Ferdinand being dead, as they thought, Sebastian would succeed to the throne on Alonso's death. And they would have carried out their wicked purpose while their victim was asleep, but that Ariel woke him in good time.

Many tricks did Ariel play them. Once he set a banquet before them, and just as they were going to fall to, he appeared to them amid thunder and

40

lightning in the form of a harpy, and immediately the banquet disappeared. Then Ariel upbraided them with their sins and vanished too.

Prospero by his enchantments drew them all to the grove without his cell, where they waited, trembling and afraid, and now at last bitterly repenting them of their sins.

Prospero determined to make one last use of his magic power, "And then," said he, "I'll break my staff and deeper than did ever plummet sound I'll drown my book."

So he made heavenly music to sound in the air, and appeared to them in his proper shape as the Duke of Milan. Because they repented, he forgave them and told them the story of his life since they had cruelly committed him and his baby daughter to the mercy of wind and waves. Alonso, who seemed sorriest of them all for his past crimes, lamented the loss of his heir. But Prospero drew back a curtain and showed them Ferdinand and Miranda playing at chess. Great was Alonso's joy to greet his loved son again, and when he heard that the fair maid with whom Ferdinand was playing

41

was Prospero's daughter, and that the young folks had plighted their troth, he said—

"Give me your hands, let grief and sorrow still embrace his heart that doth not wish you joy."

So all ended happily. The ship was safe in the harbor, and next day they all set sail for Naples, where Ferdinand and M i r a n d a were to be married. Ariel gave t h e m calm seas a n d auspicious gales; and many were the rejoicings at the wedding.

PLAYING CHESS.

Then Prospero, after many years of absence, went back to his own dukedom, where he was welcomed with great joy by his faithful subjects. He practiced the arts of magic no more, but his life was happy, and not only because he had found his own again, but chiefly because, when his bitterest foes who had

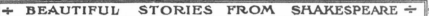

done him deadly wrong lay at his mercy, he took no vengeance on them, but nobly forgave them.

As for Ariel, Prospero made him free as air, so that he could wander where he would, and sing with a light heart his sweet song—

> " Where the bee sucks, there suck I:
> In a cowslip's bell I lie;
> There I couch when owls do cry.
> On the bat's back I do fly
> After summer, merrily:
> Merrily, merrily, shall I live now,
> Under the blossom that hangs on the bough."

ROSALIND AND CELIA.

## AS YOU LIKE IT

THERE was once a wicked Duke named Frederick, who took the dukedom that should have
belonged to his brother, sending him into exile. His
brother went into the Forest of Arden, where he
lived the life of a bold forester, as Robin Hood did
in Sherwood Forest in merry England.

44

The banished Duke's daughter, Rosalind, remained with Celia, Frederick's daughter, and the two loved each other more than most sisters. One day there was a wrestling match at Court, and Rosalind and Celia went to see it. Charles, a celebrated wrestler, was there, who had killed many men in contests of this kind. Orlando, the young man he was to wrestle with, was so slender and youthful, that Rosalind and Celia thought he would surely be killed, as others had been; so they spoke to him, and asked him not to attempt so dangerous an adventure; but the only effect of their words was to make him wish more to come off well in the encounter, so as to win praise from such sweet ladies.

Orlando, like Rosalind's father, was being kept out of his inheritance by his brother, and was so sad at his brother's unkindness that, until he saw Rosalind, he did not care much whether he lived or died. But now the sight of the fair Rosalind gave him strength and courage, so that he did marvelously, and at last, threw Charles to such a tune, that the wrestler had to be carried off the ground. Duke Frederick was pleased with his courage, and asked his name.

45

"My name is Orlando, and I am the youngest son of Sir Rowland de Boys," said the young man.

Now Sir Rowland de Boys, when he was alive, had been a good friend to the banished Duke, so that Frederick heard with regret whose son Orlando was, and would not befriend him. But Rosalind was delighted to hear that this handsome young stranger was the son of her father's old friend, and as they were going away, she turned back more than once to say another kind word to the brave young man.

"Gentleman," she said, giving him a chain from her neck, "wear this for me. I could give more, but that my hand lacks means."

Rosalind and Celia, when they were alone, began to talk about the handsome wrestler, and Rosalind confessed that she loved him at first sight.

"Come, come," said Celia, "wrestle with thy affections."

"Oh," answered Rosalind, "they take the part of a better wrestler than myself. Look, here comes the Duke."

"With his eyes full of anger," said Celia.

46

"You must leave the Court at once," he said to Rosalind. "Why?" she asked.

"Never mind why," answered the Duke, "you are banished. If within ten days you are found within twenty miles of my Court, you die."

ROSALIND GIVES ORLANDO A CHAIN.

So Rosalind set out to seek her father, the banished Duke, in the Forest of Arden. Celia loved her too much to let her go alone, and as it was rather a dangerous journey, Rosalind, being the taller, dressed up as a young countryman, and her cousin as a country girl, and Rosalind said that she would be called Ganymede, and Celia, Aliena. They were very tired when at last they came to the Forest of Arden, and as they were sitting on the grass a countryman passed that way, and Ganymede asked him if he could get them food. He did so, and told them that a shepherd's flocks and house were to be sold. They bought these and settled down as shepherd and shepherdess in the forest.

In the meantime, Oliver having sought to take his brother Orlando's life, Orlando also wandered into the forest, and there met with the rightful Duke, and being kindly received, stayed with him. Now, Orlando could think of nothing but Rosalind, and he went about the forest carving her name on trees, and writing love sonnets and hanging them on the bushes, and there Rosalind and Celia found them. One day Orlando met them, but he did not know Rosalind in her boy's clothes, though he liked the pretty shepherd youth, because he fancied a likeness in him to her he loved.

"There is a foolish lover," said Rosalind, "who haunts these woods and hangs sonnets on the trees. If I could find him, I would soon cure him of his folly."

Orlando confessed that he was the foolish lover, and Rosalind said—"If you will come and see me every day, I will pretend to be Rosalind, and I will take her part, and be wayward and contrary, as is the way of women, till I make you ashamed of your folly in loving her."

And so every day he went to her house, and took a pleasure in saying to her all the pretty things he would have said to Rosalind; and she had the fine and secret joy of knowing that all his love-words came to the right ears. Thus many days passed pleasantly away.

One morning, as Orlando was going to visit Ganymede, he saw a man asleep on the ground, and that there was a lioness crouching near, waiting for the man who was asleep to wake: for they say that lions will not prey on anything that is dead or sleeping. Then Orlando looked at the man, and saw that it was his wicked brother, Oliver, who had tried to take his life. He fought with the lioness and killed her, and saved his brother's life.

While Orlando was fighting the lioness, Oliver woke to see his brother, whom he had treated so

49

badly, saving him from a wild beast at the risk of
his own life. This made him repent of his wickedness, and he begged Orlando's pardon, and from
thenceforth they were dear brothers. The lioness
had wounded Orlando's arm so much, that he could
not go on to see the shepherd, so he sent his brother
to ask Ganymede to come to him.

Oliver went and told the whole story to Ganymede and Aliena, and Aliena was so charmed with
his manly way of confessing his faults, that she fell
in love with him at once. But when Ganymede
heard of the danger Orlando had been in she
fainted; and when she came to herself, said
truly enough, "I should have been a woman by
right."

Oliver went back to his brother and told him all
this, saying, "I love Aliena so well that I will give
up my estates to you and marry her, and live here as
a shepherd."

"Let your wedding be to-morrow," said Orlando,
"and I will ask the Duke and his friends."

When Orlando told Ganymede how his brother
was to be married on the morrow, he added: "Oh,

how bitter a thing it is to look into happiness through another man's eyes."

Then answered Rosalind, still in Ganymede's dress and speaking with his voice—"If you do love

GANYMEDE FAINTS.

Rosalind so near the heart, then when your brother marries Aliena, shall you marry her."

Now the next day the Duke and his followers, and Orlando, and Oliver, and Aliena, were all gathered together for the wedding.

Then Ganymede came in and said to the Duke,

51

"If I bring in your daughter Rosalind, will you give her to Orlando here?" "That I would," said the Duke, "if I had all kingdoms to give with her."

"And you say you will have her when I bring her?" she said to Orlando. "That would I," he answered, "were I king of all kingdoms."

Then Rosalind and Celia went out, and Rosalind put on her pretty woman's clothes again, and after a while came back.

She turned to her father—"I give myself to you, for I am yours." "If there be truth in sight," he said, "you are my daughter."

Then she said to Orlando, "I give myself to you, for I am yours." "If there be truth in sight," he said, "you are my Rosalind."

"I will have no father if you be not he," she said to the Duke, and to Orlando, "I will have no husband if you be not he."

So Orlando and Rosalind were married, and Oliver and Celia, and they lived happy ever after, returning with the Duke to the kingdom. For Frederick had been shown by a holy hermit the wickedness of his ways, and so gave back the duke-

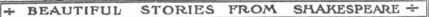

dom of his brother, and himself went into a monastery to pray for forgiveness.

The wedding was a merry one, in the mossy glades of the forest. A shepherd and shepherdess who had been friends with Rosalind, when she was herself disguised as a shepherd, were married on the same day, and all with such pretty feastings and merry-makings as could be nowhere within four walls, but only in the beautiful green wood.

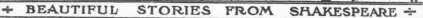

LEFT ON THE SEA-COAST.

## THE WINTER'S TALE

LEONTES was the King of Sicily, and his dearest friend was Polixenes, King of Bohemia. They had been brought up together, and only separated when they reached man's estate and each had to go and rule over his kingdom. After many years, when each was married and had a son, Polixenes came to stay with Leontes in Sicily.

Leontes was a violent-tempered man and rather silly, and he took it into his stupid head that his wife, Hermione, liked Polixenes better than she did him,

54

her own husband. When once he had got this into his head, nothing could put it out; and he ordered one of his lords, Camillo, to put a poison in Polixenes' wine. Camillo tried to dissuade him from this wicked action, but finding he was not to be moved, pretended to consent. He then told Polixenes what was proposed against him, and they fled from the Court of Sicily that night, and returned to Bohemia, where Camillo lived on as Polixenes' friend and counselor.

Leontes threw the Queen into prison; and her son, the heir to the throne, died of sorrow to see his mother so unjustly and cruelly treated.

While the Queen was in prison she had a little baby, and a friend of hers, named Paulina, had the baby dressed in its best, and took it to show the King, thinking that the sight of his helpless little daughter would soften his heart towards his dear Queen, who had never done him any wrong, and who loved him a great deal more than he deserved; but the King would not look at the baby, and ordered Paulina's husband to take it away in a ship, and leave it in the most desert and dreadful place he could find, which Paulina's husband, very much against his will, was obliged to do.

Then the poor Queen was brought up to be tried for treason in preferring Polixenes to her King; but really she had never thought of anyone except Leontes, her husband. Leontes had sent some messengers to ask the god, Apollo, whether he was not right in his cruel thoughts of the Queen. But he had not patience to wait till they came back, and so it happened that they arrived in the middle of the trial. The Oracle said—

"Hermione is innocent, Polixenes blameless, Camillo a true subject, Leontes a jealous tyrant, and the King shall live without an heir, if that which is lost be not found."

Then a man came and told them that the little Prince was dead. The poor Queen, hearing this, fell down in a fit; and then the King saw how wicked and wrong he had been. He ordered Paulina and the ladies who were with the Queen to take her away, and try to restore her. But Paulina came back in a few moments, and told the King that Hermione was dead.

56

Now Leontes' eyes were at last opened to his folly. His Queen was dead, and the little daughter who might have been a comfort to him he had sent away to be the prey of wolves and kites. Life had nothing left for him now. He gave himself up to his grief, and passed many sad years in prayer and remorse.

The baby Princess was left on the sea-coast of Bohemia, the very kingdom where Polixenes reigned.

THE KING WOULD NOT LOOK.

Paulina's husband never went home to tell Leontes where he had left the baby; for as he was going back to the ship, he met a bear and was torn to pieces. So there was an end of him.

But the poor deserted little baby was found by a

57

shepherd. She was richly dressed, and had with her some jewels, and a paper was pinned to her cloak, saying that her name was Perdita, and that she came of noble parents.

The shepherd, being a kind-hearted man, took home the little baby to his wife, and they brought it up as their own child. She had no more teaching than a shepherd's child generally has, but she inherited from her royal mother many graces and charms, so that she was quite different from the other maidens in the village where she lived.

One day Prince Florizel, the son of the good King of Bohemia, was hunting near the shepherd's house and saw Perdita, now grown up to a charming woman. He made friends with the shepherd, not telling him that he was the Prince, but saying that his name was Doricles, and that he was a private gentleman; and then, being deeply in love with the pretty Perdita, he came almost daily to see her.

The King could not understand what it was that took his son nearly every day from home; so he set people to watch him, and then found out that the heir of the King of Bohemia was in love with

Perdita, the pretty shepherd girl. Polixenes, wishing to see whether this was true, disguised himself, and went with the faithful Camillo, in disguise too, to the old shepherd's house. They arrived at the feast of sheep-shearing, and, though strangers, they were made very welcome. There was dancing going on, and a peddler was selling ribbons and laces and gloves, which the young men bought for their sweethearts.

Florizel and Perdita, however, were taking no part in this gay scene, but sat quietly together talking. The King noticed the charming manners and great beauty of Perdita, never guessing that she was the daughter of his old friend, Leontes. He said to Camillo—

"This is the prettiest low-born lass that ever ran on the green sward. Nothing she does or seems but smacks of something greater than herself—too noble for this place."

And Camillo answered, "In truth she is the Queen of curds and cream."

But when Florizel, who did not recognize his father, called upon the strangers to witness his be-

59

trothal with the pretty shepherdess, the King made himself known and forbade the marriage, adding that if ever she saw Florizel again, he would kill her and her old father, the shepherd; and with that he left them. But Camillo remained behind, for he

LEONTES RECEIVING FLORIZEL AND PERDITA.

was charmed with Perdita, and wished to befriend her.

Camillo had long known how sorry Leontes was for that foolish madness of his, and he longed to go back to Sicily to see his old master. He now proposed that the young people should go there and claim the protection of Leontes. So they went, and the shepherd went with them, taking Perdita's jewels, her baby clothes, and the paper he had found pinned to her cloak.

Leontes received them with great kindness. He was very polite to Prince Florizel, but all his looks were for Perdita. He saw how much she was like the Queen Hermione, and said again and again—

"Such a sweet creature my daughter might have been, if I had not cruelly sent her from me."

When the old shepherd heard that the King had lost a baby daughter, who had been left upon the coast of Bohemia, he felt sure that Perdita, the child he had reared, must be the King's daughter, and when he told his tale and showed the jewels and the paper, the King perceived that Perdita was indeed his long-lost child. He welcomed her with joy, and rewarded the good shepherd.

Polixenes had hastened after his son to prevent his marriage with Perdita, but when he found that she was the daughter of his old friend, he was only too glad to give his consent.

Yet Leontes could not be happy. He remembered how his fair Queen, who should have been at his side to share his joy in his daughter's happiness, was dead through his unkindness, and he could say nothing for a long time but—

"Oh, thy mother! thy mother!" and ask forgiveness of the King of Bohemia, and then kiss his daughter again, and then the Prince Florizel, and then thank the old shepherd for all his goodness.

FLORIZEL AND PERDITA TALKING.

Then Paulina, who had been high all these years in the King's favor, because of her kindness to the dead Queen Hermione, said—"I have a statue made in the likeness of the dead Queen, a piece many years in doing, and performed by the rare Italian master, Giulio Romano. I keep it in a private house apart, and there, ever since you lost your Queen, I have gone twice or thrice a day. Will it please your Majesty to go and see the statue?"

So Leontes and Polixenes, and Florizel and Perdita, with Camillo and their attendants, went to Paulina's house where there was a heavy purple curtain screening off an alcove; and Paulina, with her hand on the curtain, said—

"She was peerless when she was alive, and I do believe that her dead likeness excels whatever yet you have looked upon, or that the hand of man hath done. Therefore I keep it lonely, apart. But here it is—behold, and say, 'tis well."

And with that she drew back the curtain and showed them the statue. The King gazed and gazed on the beautiful statue of his dead wife, but said nothing.

"I like your silence," said Paulina; "it the more shows off your wonder. But speak, is it not like her?"

"It is almost herself," said the King, "and yet, Paulina, Hermione was not so much wrinkled, nothing like so old as this seems."

63

"Oh, not by much," said Polixenes.

"Ah," said Paulina, "that is the cleverness of the carver, who shows her to us as she would have been, had she lived till now."

And still Leontes looked at the statue and could not take his eyes away.

"If I had known," said Paulina, "that this poor image would so have stirred your grief, and love, I would not have shown it to you."

But he only answered, "Do not draw the curtain."

"No, you must not look any longer," said Paulina, "or you will think it moves."

"Let be! let be!" said the King. "Would you not think it breathed?"

"I will draw the curtain," said Paulina; "you will think it lives presently."

"Ah, sweet Paulina," said Leontes, "make me to think so twenty years together."

"If you can bear it," said Paulina, "I can make the statue move, make it come down and take you by the hand. Only you would think it was by wicked magic."

"Whatever you can make her do, I am content to look on," said the King.

And then, all folks there admiring and beholding, the statue moved from its pedestal, and came down the steps and put its arms round the King's neck, and he held her face and kissed her many times, for this was no statue, but the real living Queen Hermione herself. She had lived hidden, by Paulina's kind-

HERMIONE.

65

ness, all these years, and would not discover herself to her husband, though she knew he had repented, because she could not quite forgive him till she knew what had become of her little baby.

Now that Perdita was found, she forgave her husband everything, and it was like a new and beautiful marriage to them, to be together once more.

Florizel and Perdita were married and lived long and happily.

To Leontes his many years of suffering were well paid for in the moment when, after long grief and pain, he felt the arms of his true love around him once again.

CORDELIA AND THE KING OF FRANCE.

### KING LEAR

**K**ING LEAR was old and tired. He was aweary of the business of his kingdom, and wished only to end his days quietly near his three daughters. Two of his daughters were married to the Dukes of Albany and Cornwall; and the Duke of Burgundy and the King of France were both suitors for the hand of Cordelia, his youngest daughter.

Lear called his three daughters together, and told them that he proposed to divide his kingdom between

67

them. "But first," said he, "I should like to know how much you love me."

Goneril, who was really a very wicked woman, and did not love her father at all, said she loved him more than words could say; she loved him dearer than eyesight, space or liberty, more than life, grace, health, beauty, and honor.

"I love you as much as my sister and more," professed Regan, "since I care for nothing but my father's love."

Lear was very much pleased with Regan's professions, and turned to his youngest daughter, Cordelia. "Now, our joy, though last not least," he said, "the best part of my kingdom have I kept for you. What can you say?"

"Nothing, my lord," answered Cordelia.

"Nothing can come of nothing. Speak again," said the King.

And Cordelia answered, "I love your Majesty according to my duty—no more, no less."

And this she said, because she was disgusted with the way in which her sisters professed love, when really they had not even a right sense of duty to their old father.

"I am your daughter," she went on, "and you have brought me up and loved one, and I return you those duties back as are right and fit, obey you, love you, and most honor you."

GONERIL AND REGAN.

Lear, who loved Cordelia best, had wished her to make more extravagant professions of love than her sisters. "Go," he said, "be for ever a stranger to my heart and me."

The Earl of Kent, one of Lear's favorite court-

69

iers and captains, tried to say a word for Cordelia's sake, but Lear would not listen. He divided the kingdom between Goneril and Regan, and told them that he should only keep a hundred knights at arms, and would live with his daughters by turns.

When the Duke of Burgundy knew that Cordelia would have no share of the kingdom, he gave up his courtship of her. But the King of France was wiser, and said, "Thy dowerless daughter, King, is Queen of us—of ours, and our fair France."

"Take her, take her," said the King; "for I will never see that face of hers again."

So Cordelia became Queen of France, and the Earl of Kent, for having ventured to take her part, was banished from the kingdom. The King now went to stay with his daughter Goneril, who had got everything from her father that he had to give, and now began to grudge even the hundred knights that he had reserved for himself. She was harsh and undutiful to him, and her servants either refused to obey his orders or pretended that they did not hear them.

Now the Earl of Kent, when he was banished,

70

made as though he would go into another country, but instead he came back in the disguise of a serving-man and took service with the King. The King had now two friends—the Earl of Kent, whom he only knew as his servant, and his Fool, who was faithful to him. Goneril told her father plainly that his knights only served to fill her Court with riot and feasting; and so she begged him only to keep a few old men about him such as himself.

"My train are men who know all parts of duty," said Lear. "Goneril, I will not trouble you further—yet I have left another daughter."

And his horses being saddled, he set out with his followers for the castle of Regan. But she, who had formerly outdone her sister in professions of attachment to the King, now seemed to outdo her in undutiful conduct, saying that fifty knights were too many to wait on him, and Goneril (who had hurried thither to prevent Regan showing any kindness to the old King) said five were too many, since her servants could wait on him.

Then when Lear saw that what they really wanted was to drive him away, he left them. It was a wild

71

and stormy night, and he wandered about the heath half mad with misery, and with no companion but the poor Fool. But presently his servant, the good Earl of Kent, met him, and at last persuaded him to lie down in a wretched little hovel. At daybreak the Earl of Kent removed his royal master to Dover, and hurried to the Court of France to tell Cordelia what had happened.

Cordelia's husband gave her an army and with it she landed at Dover. Here she found poor King Lear, wandering about the fields, wearing a crown of nettles and weeds. They brought him back and fed and clothed him, and Cordelia came to him and kissed him.

"You must bear with me," said Lear; "forget and forgive. I am old and foolish."

And now he knew at last which of his children it was that had loved him best, and who was worthy of his love.

Goneril and Regan joined their armies to fight Cordelia's army, and were successful; and Cordelia and her father were thrown into prison. Then Goneril's husband, the Duke of Albany, who was a good man, and had not known how wicked his wife was, heard the truth of the whole story; and when Goneril found that her husband knew her for the wicked woman she was, she killed herself, having a little time before given a deadly poison to her sister, Regan, out of a spirit of jealousy.

But they had arranged that Cordelia should be hanged in prison, and though the Duke of Albany sent messengers at once, it was too late. The old King came

CORDELIA IN PRISON.

staggering into the tent of the Duke of Albany, carrying the body of his dear daughter Cordelia in his arms.

And soon after, with words of love for her upon his lips, he fell with her still in his arms, and died.

VIOLA AND THE CAPTAIN.

## TWELFTH NIGHT

ORSINO, the Duke of Illyria, was deeply in
love with a beautiful Countess named Olivia.
Yet was all his love in vain, for she disdained his
suit; and when her brother died, she sent back a messenger from the Duke, bidding him tell his master
that for seven years she would not let the very air
behold her face, but that, like a nun, she would
walk veiled; and all this for the sake of a dead
brother's love, which she would keep fresh and last-
ing in her sad remembrance.

74

The Duke longed for someone to whom he could tell his sorrow, and repeat over and over again the story of his love. And chance brought him such a companion. For about this time a goodly ship was wrecked on the Illyrian coast, and among those who reached land in safety were the captain and a fair young maid, named Viola. But she was little grateful for being rescued from the perils of the sea, since she feared that her twin brother was drowned, Sebastian, as dear to her as the heart in her bosom, and so like her that, but for the difference in their manner of dress, one could hardly be told from the other. The captain, for her comfort, told her that he had seen her brother bind himself "to a strong mast that lived upon the sea," and that thus there was hope that he might be saved.

Viola now asked in whose country she was, and learning that the young Duke Orsino ruled there, and was as noble in his nature as in his name, she decided to disguise herself in male attire, and seek for employment with him as a page.

In this she succeeded, and now from day to day she had to listen to the story of Orsino's love. At

75

first she sympathized very truly with him, but soon
her sympathy grew to love. At last it occurred
to Orsino that his hopeless love-suit might prosper
better if he sent this pretty lad to woo Olivia for

VIOLA AS "CESARIO" MEETS OLIVIA.

him. Viola unwillingly went on this errand, but
when she came to the house, Malvolio, Olivia's steward, a vain, officious man, sick, as his mistress told
him, of self-love, forbade the messenger admittance.

76

Viola, however (who was now called Cesario), refused to take any denial, and vowed to have speech with the Countess. Olivia, hearing how her instructions were defied and curious to see this daring youth, said, "We'll once more hear Orsino's embassy."

When Viola was admitted to her presence and the servants had been sent away, she listened patiently to the reproaches which this bold messenger from the Duke poured upon her, and listening she fell in love with the supposed Cesario; and when Cesario had gone, Olivia longed to send some love-token after him. So, calling Malvolio, she bade him follow the boy.

"He left this ring behind him," she said, taking one from her finger. "Tell him I will none of it."

Malvolio did as he was bid, and then Viola, who of course knew perfectly well that she had left no ring behind her, saw with a woman's quickness that Olivia loved her. Then she went back to the Duke, very sad at heart for her lover, and for Olivia, and for herself.

It was but cold comfort she could give Orsino,

who now sought to ease the pangs of despised love by listening to sweet music, while Cesario stood by his side.

"Ah," said the Duke to his page that night, "you too have been in love."

"A little," answered Viola.

"YOU TOO HAVE BEEN IN LOVE."

"What kind of woman is it?" he asked.

"Of your complexion," she answered.

"What years, i' faith?" was his next question.

To this came the pretty answer, "About your years, my lord."

78

"Too old, by Heaven!" cried the Duke. "Let still the woman take an elder than herself."

And Viola very meekly said, "I think it well, my lord."

By and by Orsino begged Cesario once more to visit Olivia and to plead his love-suit. But she, thinking to dissuade him, said—

"If some lady loved you as you love Olivia?"

"Ah! that cannot be," said the Duke.

"But I know," Viola went on, "what love woman may have for a man. My father had a daughter loved a man, as it might be," she added blushing, "perhaps, were I a woman, I should love your lordship."

"And what is her history?" he asked.

"A blank, my lord," Viola answered. "She never told her love, but let concealment like a worm in the bud feed on her damask cheek: she pined in thought, and with a green and yellow melancholy she sat, like Patience on a monument, smiling at grief. Was not this love indeed?"

"But died thy sister of her love, my boy?" the Duke asked; and Viola, who had all the time been

79

telling her own love for him in this pretty fashion, said—

"I am all the daughters my father has and all the brothers—Sir, shall I go to the lady?"

"To her in haste," said the Duke, at once forgetting all about the story, "and give her this jewel."

So Viola went, and this time poor Olivia was unable to hide her love, and openly confessed it with such passionate truth, that Viola left her hastily, saying—

"Nevermore will I deplore my master's tears to you."

But in vowing this, Viola did not know the tender pity she would feel for other's suffering. So when Olivia, in the violence of her love, sent a messenger, praying Cesario to visit her once more, Cesario had no heart to refuse the request.

But the favors which Olivia bestowed upon this mere page aroused the jealousy of Sir Andrew Aguecheek, a foolish, rejected lover of hers, who at that time was staying at her house with her merry old uncle Sir Toby. This same Sir Toby dearly loved a practical joke, and knowing Sir Andrew to be an arrant coward, he thought that if he could bring off a duel between him and Cesario, there would be rare sport indeed. So he induced Sir Andrew to send a challenge, which he himself took to Cesario. The poor page, in great terror, said—

"I will return again to the house, I am no fighter."

"Back you shall not to the house," said Sir Toby, "unless you fight me first."

And as he looked a very fierce old gentleman, Viola thought it best to await Sir Andrew's coming; and when he at last made his appearance, in a great fright, if the truth had been known, she tremblingly drew her sword, and Sir Andrew in like fear followed her example. Happily for them both, at this moment some officers of the Court came on the scene, and stopped the intended duel. Viola gladly made off with what speed she might, while Sir Toby called after her—

"A very paltry boy, and more a coward than a hare!"

Now, while these things were happening, Sebastian had escaped all the dangers of the deep, and had landed safely in Illyria, where he determined to make his way to the Duke's Court. On his way thither he passed Olivia's house just as Viola had left it in such a hurry, and whom should he meet but Sir Andrew and Sir Toby. Sir Andrew, mistaking Sebastian for the cowardly Cesario, took his courage in both hands, and walking up to him struck him, saying, "There's for you."

"Why, there's for you; and there, and there!" said Sebastian, hitting back a great deal harder, and again and again, till Sir Toby came to the rescue of his friend. Sebastian, however, tore himself free from Sir Toby's clutches, and drawing his sword would have fought them both, but that Olivia herself, having heard of the quarrel, came running in, and with many reproaches sent Sir Toby and his friend away. Then turning to Sebastian, whom she too thought to be Cesario, she besought him with many a pretty speech to come into the house with her.

Sebastian, half dazed and all delighted with her beauty and grace, readily consented, and that very day, so great was Olivia's haste, they were married before she had discovered that he was not Cesario, or

Sebastian was quite certain whether or not he was in a dream.

Meanwhile Orsino, hearing how ill Cesario sped with Olivia, visited her himself, taking Cesario with him. Olivia met them both before her door, and seeing, as she thought, her husband there, reproached him for leaving her, while to the Duke she said that his suit was as fat and wholesome to her as howling after music.

"Still so cruel?" said Orsino.

"Still so constant," she answered.

Then Orsino's anger growing to cruelty, he vowed that, to be revenged on her, he would kill Cesario, whom he knew she loved. "Come, boy," he said to the page.

And Viola, following him as he moved away, said, "I, to do you rest, a thousand deaths would die."

A great fear took hold on Olivia, and she cried aloud, "Cesario, husband, stay!"

"Her husband?" asked the Duke angrily.

"No, my lord, not I," said Viola.

"Call forth the holy father," cried Olivia.

And the priest who had married Sebastian and

Olivia, coming in, declared Cesario to be the bride-groom.

"O thou dissembling cub!" the Duke exclaimed. "Farewell, and take her, but go where thou and I henceforth may never meet."

At this moment Sir Andrew came up with bleeding crown, complaining that Cesario had broken his head, and Sir Toby's as well.

"I never hurt you," said Viola, very positively; "you drew your sword on me, but I bespoke you fair, and hurt you not."

Yet, for all her protesting, no one there believed her; but all their thoughts were on a sudden changed to wonder, when Sebastian came in.

"I am sorry, madam," he said to his wife, "I have hurt your kinsman. Pardon me, sweet, even for the vows we made each other so late ago."

"One face, one voice, one habit, and two persons!" cried the Duke, looking first at Viola, and then at Sebastian.

"An apple cleft in two," said one who knew Sebastian, "is not more twin than these two creatures. Which is Sebastian?"

"I never had a brother," said Sebastian. "I had a sister, whom the blind waves and surges have devoured." "Were you a woman," he said to Viola, "I should let my tears fall upon your cheek, and say, 'Thrice welcome, drowned Viola!'"

Then Viola, rejoicing to see her dear brother alive, confessed that she was indeed his sister, Viola. As she spoke, Orsino felt the pity that is akin to love.

"Boy," he said, "thou hast said to me a thousand times thou never shouldst love woman like to me."

"And all those sayings will I overswear," Viola replied, "and all those swearings keep true."

"Give me thy hand," Orsino cried in gladness. "Thou shalt be my wife, and my fancy's queen."

Thus was the gentle Viola made happy, while Olivia found in Sebastian a constant lover, and a good husband, and he in her a true and loving wife.

CLAUDIO AND HERO.

## MUCH ADO ABOUT NOTHING

IN Sicily is a town called Messina, which is the scene of a curious storm in a teacup that raged several hundred years ago.

It began with sunshine. Don Pedro, Prince of Arragon, in Spain, had gained so complete a victory over his foes that the very land whence they came is forgotten. Feeling happy and playful after the fatigues of war, Don Pedro came for a

86

holiday to Messina, and in his suite were his step-brother Don John and two young Italian lords, Benedick and Claudio.

Benedick was a merry chatterbox, who had determined to live a bachelor. Claudio, on the other hand, no sooner arrived at Messina than he fell in love with Hero, the daughter of Leonato, Governor of Messina.

One July day, a perfumer called Borachio was burning dried lavender in a musty room in Leonato's house, when the sound of conversation floated through the open window.

"Give me your candid opinion of Hero," Claudio asked, and Borachio settled himself for comfortable listening.

"Too short and brown for praise," was Benedick's reply; "but alter her color or height, and you spoil her."

"In my eyes she is the sweetest of women," said Claudio.

"Not in mine," retorted Benedick, "and I have no need for glasses. She is like the last day of December compared with the first of May if you set her beside her cousin. Unfortunately, the Lady Beatrice is a fury."

Beatrice was Leonato's niece. She amused herself by saying witty and severe things about Benedick, who called her Dear Lady Disdain. She was wont to say that she was born under a dancing star, and could not therefore be dull.

Claudio and Benedick were still talking when Don Pedro came up and said good-humoredly, "Well, gentlemen, what's the secret?"

"I am longing," answered Benedick, "for your Grace to command me to tell."

"I charge you, then, on your allegiance to tell me," said Don Pedro, falling in with his humor.

"I can be as dumb as a mute," apologized Benedick to Claudio, "but his Grace commands my speech." To Don Pedro he said, "Claudio is in love with Hero, Leonato's short daughter."

Don Pedro was pleased, for he admired Hero and was fond of Claudio. When Benedick had departed, he said to Claudio, "Be steadfast in your love for Hero, and I will help you to win her. To-night her father gives a masquerade, and I will pretend I am Claudio, and tell her how Claudio loves her, and if she be pleased, I will go to her father and ask his consent to your union."

Most men like to do their own wooing, but if you fall in love with a Governor's only daughter, you are fortunate if you can trust a prince to plead for you.

Claudio then was fortunate, but he was unfortunate as well, for he had an enemy who was outwardly a friend. This enemy was Don Pedro's stepbrother Don John, who was jealous of Claudio because Don Pedro preferred him to Don John.

It was to Don John that Borachio came with the interesting conversation which he had overheard.

"I shall have some fun at that masquerade myself," said Don John when Borachio ceased speaking.

On the night of the masquerade, Don Pedro, masked and pretending he was Claudio, asked Hero if he might walk with her.

They moved away together, and Don John went up to Claudio and said, "Signor Benedick, I believe?"

"The same," fibbed Claudio.

"I should be much obliged then," said Don John, "if you would use your influence with my brother to cure him of his love for Hero. She is beneath him in rank."

"How do you know he loves her?" inquired Claudio.

"I heard him swear his affection," was the reply, and Borachio chimed in with, "So did I too."

Claudio was then left to himself, and

HERO AND URSULA.

his thought was that his Prince had betrayed him. "Farewell, Hero," he muttered; "I was a fool to trust to an agent."

Meanwhile Beatrice and Benedick (who was

masked) were having a brisk exchange of opinions.

"Did Benedick ever make you laugh?" asked she.

"Who is Benedick?" he inquired.

"A Prince's jester," replied Beatrice, and she spoke so sharply that "I would not marry her," he declared afterwards, "if her estate were the Garden of Eden."

But the principal speaker at the masquerade was neither Beatrice nor Benedick. It was Don Pedro, who carried out his plan to the letter, and brought the light back to Claudio's face in a twinkling, by appearing before him with Leonato and Hero, and saying, "Claudio, when would you like to go to church?"

"To-morrow," was the prompt answer. "Time goes on crutches till I marry Hero."

"Give her a week, my dear son," said Leonato, and Claudio's heart thumped with joy.

"And now," said the amiable Don Pedro, "we must find a wife for Signor Benedick. It is a task for Hercules."

"I will help you," said Leonato, "if I have to sit up ten nights."

Then Hero spoke. "I will do what I can, my lord, to find a good husband for Beatrice."

Thus, with happy laughter, ended the masquerade which had given Claudio a lesson for nothing.

Borachio cheered up Don John by laying a plan before him with which he was confident he could persuade both Claudio and Don Pedro that Hero was a fickle girl who had two strings to her bow. Don John agreed to this plan of hate.

Don Pedro, on the other hand, had devised a cunning plan of love. "If," he said to Leonato, "we pretend, when Beatrice is near enough to overhear us, that Benedick is pining for her love, she will pity him, see his good qualities, and love him. And if, when Benedick thinks we don't know he is listening, we say how sad it is that the beautiful Beatrice should be in love with a heartless scoffer like Benedick, he will certainly be on his knees before her in a week or less."

So one day, when Benedick was reading in a summer-house, Claudio sat down outside it with Leonato, and said, "Your daughter told me something about a letter she wrote."

92

"Letter!" exclaimed Leonato. "She will get up twenty times in the night and write goodness knows what. But once Hero peeped, and saw the words 'Benedick and Beatrice' on the sheet, and then Beatrice tore it up."

"Hero told me," said Claudio, "that she cried, 'O sweet Benedick!'"

Benedick was touched to the core by this improbable story, which he was vain enough to believe. "She is fair and good," he said to himself. "I must not seem proud. I feel that I love her. People will laugh, of course; but their paper bullets will do me no harm."

At this moment Beatrice came to the summer-house, and said, "Against my will, I have come to tell you that dinner is ready."

"Fair Beatrice, I thank you," said Benedick.

"I took no more pains to come than you take pains to thank me," was the rejoinder, intended to freeze him.

But it did not freeze him. It warmed him. The meaning he squeezed out of her rude speech was that she was delighted to come to him.

93

Hero, who had undertaken the task of melting the heart of Beatrice, took no trouble to seek an occasion. She simply said to her maid Margaret one day, "Run into the parlor and whisper to Beatrice that Ursula and I are talking about her in the orchard."

Having said this, she felt as sure that Beatrice would overhear what was meant for her ears as if she had made an appointment with her cousin.

In the orchard was a bower, screened from the sun by honeysuckles, and Beatrice entered it a few minutes after Margaret had gone on her errand.

BENEDICK.

"But are you sure," asked Ursula, who was one of Hero's attendants, "that Benedick loves Beatrice so devotedly?"

94

*Sitven Sculp.*

From Mr Ozias Humphry's Drawing of the
Chandos Picture made for the late Mr Malone
in the Year 1783.

**WILLIAM SHAKESPEARE**

TITANIA AND THE CLOWN

FERDINAND AND MIRANDA

PRINCE FLORIZEL AND PERDITA

ROMEO AND JULIET

IMOGEN

CHOOSING THE CASKET

PETRUCHIO AND KATHERINE

"So say the Prince and my betrothed," replied Hero, "and they wished me to tell her, but I said, 'No! Let Benedick get over it.' "

"Why did you say that?"

"Because Beatrice is unbearably proud. Her eyes sparkle with disdain and scorn. She is too conceited to love. I should not like to see her making game of poor Benedick's love. I would rather see Benedick waste away like a covered fire."

"I don't agree with you," said Ursula. "I think your cousin is too clear-sighted not to see the merits of Benedick." "He is the one man in Italy, except Claudio," said Hero.

The talkers then left the orchard, and Beatrice, excited and tender, stepped out of the summer-house, saying to herself, "Poor dear Benedick, be true to me, and your love shall tame this wild heart of mine."

We now return to the plan of hate.

The night before the day fixed for Claudio's wedding, Don John entered a room in which Don Pedro and Claudio were conversing, and asked Claudio if he intended to be married to-morrow.

95

"You know he does!" said Don Pedro.

"He may know differently," said Don John, "when he has seen what I will show him if he will follow me."

They followed him into the garden; and they saw a lady leaning out of Hero's window talking love to Borachio.

Claudio thought the lady was Hero, and said, "I will shame her for it to-morrow!" Don Pedro thought she was Hero, too; but she was not Hero; she was Margaret.

Don John chuckled noiselessly when Claudio and Don Pedro quitted the garden; he gave Borachio a purse containing a thousand ducats.

The money made Borachio feel very gay, and when he was walking in the street with his friend Conrade, he boasted of his wealth and the giver, and told what he had done.

A watchman overheard them, and thought that a man who had been paid a thousand ducats for villainy was worth taking in charge. He therefore arrested Borachio and Conrade, who spent the rest of the night in prison.

Before noon of the next day half the aristocrats in Messina were at church. Hero thought it was her wedding day, and she was there in her wedding dress, no cloud on her pretty face or in her frank and shining eyes.

The priest was Friar Francis.

Turning to Claudio, he said, "You come hither, my lord, to marry this lady?" "No!" contradicted Claudio.

Leonato thought he was quibbling over grammar. "You should have said, Friar," said he, " 'You come to be married to her.' "

Friar Francis turned to Hero. "Lady," he said, "you come hither to be married to this Count?" "I do," replied Hero.

"If either of you know any impediment to this marriage, I charge you to utter it," said the Friar.

"Do you know of any, Hero?" asked Claudio. "None," said she.

"Know you of any, Count?" demanded the Friar. "I dare reply for him, 'None,' " said Leonato.

Claudio exclaimed bitterly, "O! what will not men dare say! Father," he continued, "will you

97

give me your daughter?" "As freely," replied Leonato, "as God gave her to me."

"And what can I give you," asked Claudio, "which is worthy of this gift?" "Nothing," said Don Pedro, "unless you give the gift back to the giver."

"Sweet Prince, you teach me," said Claudio. "There, Leonato, take her back."

These brutal words were followed by others which flew from Claudio, Don Pedro and Don John.

The church seemed no longer sacred. Hero took her own part as long as she could, then she swooned. All her persecutors left the church, except her father, who was befooled by the accusations against her, and cried, "Hence from her! Let her die!"

But Friar Francis saw Hero blameless with his clear eyes that probed the soul. "She is innocent," he said; "a thousand signs have told me so."

Hero revived under his kind gaze. Her father, flurried and angry, knew not what to think, and the Friar said, "They have left her as one dead with shame. Let us pretend that she is dead until the truth is declared, and slander turns to remorse."

"The Friar advises well," said Benedick. Then Hero was led away into a retreat, and Beatrice and Benedick remained alone in the church.

Benedick knew she had been weeping bitterly and long. "Surely I do believe your fair cousin is wronged," he said. She still wept.

"Is it not strange," asked Benedick, gently, "that I love nothing in the world as well as you?"

"It were as possible for me to say I loved nothing as well as you," said Beatrice, "but I do not say it. I am sorry for my cousin."

"Tell me what to do for her," said Benedick. "Kill Claudio."

"Ha! not for the wide world," said Benedick. "Your refusal kills me," said Beatrice. "Farewell."

"Enough! I will challenge him," cried Benedick.

During this scene Borachio and Conrade were in prison. There they were examined by a constable called Dogberry.

The watchman gave evidence to the effect that Borachio had said that he had received a thousand ducats for conspiring against Hero.

Leonato was not present at this examination, but

he was nevertheless now thoroughly convinced of Hero's innocence. He played the part of bereaved father very well, and when Don Pedro and Claudio called on him in a friendly way, he said to the Italian, "You have slandered my child to death, and I challenge you to combat."

"I cannot fight an old man," said Claudio.

"You could kill a girl," sneered Leonato, and Claudio crimsoned.

Hot words grew from hot words, and both Don Pedro and Claudio were feeling scorched when Leonato left the room and Benedick entered.

"The old man," said Claudio, "was like to have snapped my nose off."

"You are a villain!" said Benedick, shortly. "Fight me when and with what weapon you please, or I call you a coward."

Claudio was astounded, but said, "I'll meet you. Nobody shall say I can't carve a calf's head."

Benedick smiled, and as it was time for Don Pedro to receive officials, the Prince sat down in a chair of state and prepared his mind for justice.

The door soon opened to admit Dogberry and his prisoners.

100

"What offence," said Don Pedro, "are these men charged with?"

Borachio thought the moment a happy one for making a clean breast of it. He laid the whole blame on Don John, who had disappeared. "The lady Hero being dead," he said, "I desire nothing but the reward of a murderer."

Claudio heard with anguish and deep repentance.

Upon the re-entrance of Leonato he said to him, "This slave makes clear your daughter's innocence. Choose your revenge."

FRIAR FRANCIS.

"Leonato," said Don Pedro, humbly, "I am ready for any penance you may impose."

"I ask you both, then," said Leonato, "to proclaim my daughter's innocence, and to honor her tomb by singing her praise before it. As for you, Claudio, I have this to say: my brother has a daughter so like Hero that she might be a copy of her. Marry her, and my vengeful feelings die."

"Noble sir," said Claudio, "I am yours." Claudio then went to his room and composed a solemn song. Going to the church with Don Pedro and his attendants, he sang it before the monument of Leonato's family. When he had ended he said, "Good night, Hero. Yearly will I do this."

He then gravely, as became a gentleman whose heart was Hero's, made ready to marry a girl whom he did not love. He was told to meet her in Leonato's house, and was faithful to his appointment.

He was shown into a room where Antonio (Leonato's brother) and several masked ladies entered after him. Friar Francis, Leonato, and Benedick were present.

Antonio led one of the ladies towards Claudio.

"Sweet," said the young man, "let me see your face."

"Swear first to marry her," said Leonato.

"Give me your hand," said Claudio to the lady; "before this holy friar I swear to marry you if you will be my wife."

"Alive I was your wife," said the lady, as she drew off her mask.

"Another Hero!" exclaimed Claudio.

"Hero died," explained Leonato, "only while slander lived."

The Friar was then going to marry the reconciled pair, but Benedick interrupted him with, "Softly, Friar; which of these ladies is Beatrice?"

Hereat Beatrice unmasked, and Benedick said, "You love me, don't you?"

"Only moderately," was the reply. "Do you love me?"

"Moderately," answered Benedick.

"I was told you were well-nigh dead for me," re-marked Beatrice.

"Of you I was told the same," said Benedick.

"Here's your own hand in evidence of your love," said Claudio, producing a feeble sonnet which Bene-dick had written to his sweetheart.

"And here," said Hero, "is a tribute to Benedick, which I picked out of the pocket of Beatrice."

"A miracle!" exclaimed Benedick. "Our hands are against our hearts! Come, I will marry you, Beatrice."

"You shall be my husband to save your life," was the rejoinder.

Benedick kissed her on the mouth; and the Friar married them after he had married Claudio and Hero.

"How is Benedick the married man?" asked Don Pedro.

"Too happy to be made unhappy," replied Benedick. "Crack what jokes you will. As for you, Claudio, I had hoped to run you through the body, but as you are now my kinsman, live whole and love my cousin."

"My cudgel was in love with you, Benedick, until to-day," said Claudio; but, "Come, come, let's dance," said Benedick.

And dance they did. Not even the news of the capture of Don John was able to stop the flying feet of the happy lovers, for revenge is not sweet against an evil man who has failed to do harm.

ROMEO AND TYBALT FIGHT.

## ROMEO AND JULIET

ONCE upon a time there lived in Verona two great families named Montagu and Capulet. They were both rich, and I suppose they were as sensible, in most things, as other rich people. But in one thing they were extremely silly. There was an old, old quarrel between the two families, and instead of making it up like reasonable folks, they made a sort of pet of their quarrel, and would not let it die out. So that a Montagu wouldn't speak to a Capulet if he met one in the street—nor a Capulet to a Montagu—or if they did speak, it was to say rude and unpleasant things, which often

105

ended in a fight. And their relations and servants were just as foolish, so that street fights and duels and uncomfortablenesses of that kind were always growing out of the Montagu-and-Capulet quarrel.

Now Lord Capulet, the head of that family, gave a party—a grand supper and a dance—and he was so hospitable that he said anyone might come to it *except* (of course) the Montagues. But there was a young Montagu named Romeo, who very much wanted to be there, because Rosaline, the lady he loved, had been asked. This lady had never been at all kind to him, and he had no reason to love her; but the fact was that he wanted to love *somebody,* and as he hadn't seen the right lady, he was obliged to love the wrong one. So to the Capulet's grand party he came, with his friends Mercutio and Benvolio.

Old Capulet welcomed him and his two friends very kindly—and young Romeo moved about among the crowd of courtly folk dressed in their velvets and satins, the men with jeweled sword hilts and collars, and the ladies with brilliant gems on breast and arms, and stones of price set in their bright girdles. Romeo was in his best too, and though he wore a black mask over his eyes and nose, everyone could see by his mouth and his hair, and the way he held his head, that he was twelve times handsomer than anyone else in the room.

Presently amid the dancers he saw a lady so beautiful and so lovable that from that moment he never again gave one thought to that Rosaline whom he had thought he loved. And he looked at this other fair lady, as she moved in the dance in her white satin and pearls, and all the world seemed vain and worthless to him compared with her. And he was saying this, or something like it, when Tybalt, Lady Capulet's nephew, hearing his voice, knew him to be Romeo. Tybalt, being very angry, went at once to his uncle, and told him how a Montagu had come uninvited to the feast; but old Capulet was too fine a gentleman to be discourteous to any man under his own roof, and he bade Tybalt be quiet. But this young man only waited for a chance to quarrel with Romeo.

In the meantime Romeo made his way to the fair lady, and told her in sweet words that he loved

her, and kissed her.   Just then her mother sent for
her, and then Romeo found out that the lady on
whom he had set his heart's hopes was Juliet, the
daughter of Lord Capulet, his sworn foe.   So he

ROMEO DISCOVERS JULIET.

went away, sorrowing indeed, but loving her none
the less.

Then Juliet said to her nurse:

"Who is that gentleman that would not dance?"

108

"His name is Romeo, and a Montagu, the only son of your great enemy," answered the nurse.

Then Juliet went to her room, and looked out of her window, over the beautiful green-grey garden, where the moon was shining. And Romeo was hidden in that garden among the trees—because he could not bear to go right away without trying to see her again. So she—not knowing him to be there—spoke her secret thought aloud, and told the quiet garden how she loved Romeo.

And Romeo heard and was glad beyond measure. Hidden below, he looked up and saw her fair face in the moonlight, framed in the blossoming creepers that grew round her window, and as he looked and listened, he felt as though he had been carried away in a dream, and set down by some magician in that beautiful and enchanted garden.

"Ah—why are you called Romeo?" said Juliet. "Since I love you, what does it matter what you are called?"

"Call me but love, and I'll be new baptized— henceforth I never will be Romeo," he cried, stepping into the full white moonlight from the shade of the cypresses and oleanders that had hidden him. She was frightened at first, but when she saw that it was Romeo himself, and no stranger, she too was glad, and, he standing in the garden below and she leaning from the window, they spoke long together, each one trying to find the sweetest words in the world, to make that pleasant talk that lovers use. And the tale of all they said, and the sweet music their voices made together, is all set down in a golden book, where you children may read it for yourselves some day.

And the time passed so quickly, as it does for folk who love each other and are together, that when the time came to part, it seemed as though they had met but that moment—and indeed they hardly knew how to part.

"I will send to you to-morrow," said Juliet.

And so at last, with lingering and longing, they said good-bye.

Juliet went into her room, and a dark curtain hid her bright window. Romeo went away through the still and dewy garden like a man in a dream.

The next morning, very early, Romeo went to

Friar Laurence, a priest, and, telling him all the story, begged him to marry him to Juliet without delay. And this, after some talk, the priest consented to do.

So when Juliet sent her old nurse to Romeo that day to know what he purposed to do, the old woman took back a message that all was well, and all things ready for the marriage of Juliet and Romeo on the next morning.

MARRIAGE OF ROMEO AND JULIET.

The young lovers were afraid to ask their parents' consent to their marriage, as young people should do, because of this foolish old quarrel between the Capulets and the Montagues.

And Friar Laurence was willing to help the young lovers secretly, because he thought that when

111

they were once married their parents might soon be told, and that the match might put a happy end to the old quarrel.

So the next morning early, Romeo and Juliet were married at Friar Laurence's cell, and parted with tears and kisses. And Romeo promised to come into the garden that evening, and the nurse got ready a rope-ladder to let down from the window, so that Romeo could climb up and talk to his dear wife quietly and alone.

But that very day a dreadful thing happened.

Tybalt, the young man who had been so vexed at Romeo's going to the Capulet's feast, met him and his two friends, Mercutio and Benvolio, in the street, called Romeo a villain, and asked him to fight. Romeo had no wish to fight with Juliet's cousin, but Mercutio drew his sword, and he and Tybalt fought. And Mercutio was killed. When Romeo saw that this friend was dead, he forgot everything except anger at the man who had killed him, and he and Tybalt fought till Tybalt fell dead.

So, on the very day of his wedding, Romeo killed

his dear Juliet's cousin, and was sentenced to be banished. Poor Juliet and her young husband met that night indeed; he climbed the rope-ladder among the flowers, and found her window, but their meeting was a sad one, and they parted with bitter tears and hearts heavy, because they could not know when they should meet again.

Now Juliet's father, who, of course, had no idea that she was married, wished her to wed a gentleman named Paris, and was so angry when she refused, that she hurried away to ask Friar Laurence what she should do. He advised her to pretend to consent, and then he said:

"I will give you a draught that will make you seem to be dead for two days, and then when they take you to church it will be to bury you, and not to marry you. They will put you in the vault thinking you are dead, and before you wake up Romeo and I will be there to take care of you. Will you do this, or are you afraid?"

"I will do it; talk not to me of fear!" said Juliet. And she went home and told her father she would marry Paris. If she had spoken out and told her father the truth . . . well, then this would have been a different story.

Lord Capulet was very much pleased to get his own way, and set about inviting his friends and getting the wedding feast ready. Everyone stayed up all night, for there was a great deal to do, and very little time to do it in. Lord Capulet was anxious to get Juliet married because he saw she was very unhappy. Of course she was really fretting about her husband Romeo, but her father thought she was grieving for the death of her cousin Tybalt, and he thought marriage would give her something else to think about.

Early in the morning the nurse came to call Juliet, and to dress her for her wedding; but she would not wake, and at last the nurse cried out suddenly—

"Alas! alas! help! help! my lady's dead! Oh, well-a-day that ever I was born!"

Lady Capulet came running in, and then Lord Capulet, and Lord Paris, the bridegroom. There lay Juliet cold and white and lifeless, and all their weeping could not wake her. So it was a burying that day instead of a marrying. Meantime Friar

114

Laurence had sent a messenger to Mantua with a letter to Romeo telling him of all these things; and all would have been well, only the messenger was delayed, and could not go.

But ill news travels fast. Romeo's servant who knew the secret of the marriage, but not of Juliet's pretended death, heard of her funeral, and hurried to Mantua to tell Romeo how his young wife was dead and lying in the grave.

THE NURSE THINKS JULIET DEAD.

"Is it so?" cried Romeo, heart-broken. "Then I will lie by Juliet's side to-night."

And he bought himself a poison, and went straight back to Verona. He hastened to the tomb where Juliet was lying. It was not a grave, but a

115

vault. He broke open the door, and was just going down the stone steps that led to the vault where all the dead Capulets lay, when he heard a voice behind him calling on him to stop.

It was the Count Paris, who was to have married Juliet that very day.

"How dare you come here and disturb the dead bodies of the Capulets, you vile Montagu?" cried Paris.

Poor Romeo, half mad with sorrow, yet tried to answer gently.

"You were told," said Paris, "that if you returned to Verona you must die."

"I must indeed," said Romeo. "I came here for nothing else. Good, gentle youth—leave me! Oh, go—before I do you any harm! I love you better than myself—go—leave me here—"

Then Paris said, "I defy you, and I arrest you as a felon," and Romeo, in his anger and despair, drew his sword. They fought, and Paris was killed.

As Romeo's sword pierced him, Paris cried—

"Oh, I am slain! If thou be merciful, open the tomb, and lay me with Juliet!"

And Romeo said, "In faith I will."

And he carried the dead man into the tomb and laid him by the dear Juliet's side.   Then he kneeled by Juliet and spoke to her, and held her in his arms, and kissed her cold lips, believing that she was dead, while all the while she was coming nearer and nearer to the time of her awaken- ing.  Then he drank the poi- son, and died beside his sweetheart and wife.

Now came Friar Lau- rence when it was too late, and saw all that had hap-

ROMEO ENTERING THE TOMB.

117

pened—and then poor Juliet woke out of her sleep to find her husband and her friend both dead beside her.

The noise of the fight had brought other folks to the place too, and Friar Laurence, hearing them, ran away, and Juliet was left alone. She saw the cup that had held the poison, and knew how all had happened, and since no poison was left for her, she drew her Romeo's dagger and thrust it through her heart—and so, falling with her head on her Romeo's breast, she died. And here ends the story of these faithful and most unhappy lovers.

\* \* \* \* \* \* \*

And when the old folks knew from Friar Laurence of all that had befallen, they sorrowed exceedingly, and now, seeing all the mischief their wicked quarrel had wrought, they repented them of it, and over the bodies of their dead children they clasped hands at last, in friendship and forgiveness.

### PERICLES

PERICLES, the Prince of Tyre, was unfortunate enough to make an enemy of Antiochus, the powerful and wicked King of Antioch; and so great was the danger in which he stood that, on the advice of his trusty counselor, Lord Helicanus, he determined to travel about the world for a time. He came to this decision despite the fact that, by the death of his father, he was now King of Tyre. So he set sail for Tarsus, appointing Helicanus Regent during his absence. That he did wisely in thus leaving his kingdom was soon made clear.

Hardly had he sailed on his voyage, when Lord Thaliard arrived from Antioch with instructions from his royal master to kill Pericles. The faithful Helicanus soon discovered the deadly purpose of this wicked lord, and at once sent messengers to Tarsus to warn the King of the danger which threatened him.

119

The people of Tarsus were in such poverty and distress that Pericles, feeling that he could find no safe refuge there, put to sea again. But a dreadful storm overtook the ship in which he was, and the good vessel was wrecked, while of all on board only Pericles was saved. Bruised and wet and faint, he was flung upon the cruel rocks on the coast of Pentapolis, the country of the good King Simonides. Worn out as he was, he looked for nothing but death, and that speedily. But some fishermen, coming down to the beach, found him there, and gave him clothes and bade him be of good cheer.

"Thou shalt come home with me," said one of them, "and we will have flesh for holidays, fish for fasting days, and moreo'er, puddings and flapjacks, and thou shalt be welcome."

They told him that on the morrow many princes and knights were going to the King's Court, there to joust and tourney for the love of his daughter, the beautiful Princess Thaisa.

"Did but my fortunes equal my desires," said Pericles, "I'd wish to make one there."

As he spoke, some of the fishermen came by, drawing their net, and it dragged heavily, resisting all their efforts, but at last they hauled it in, to find that it contained a suit of rusty armor; and looking at it, he blessed Fortune for her kindness, for he saw that it was his own, which had been given to him by his dead father. He begged the fishermen to let him have it that he might go to Court and take part in the tournament, promising that if ever his ill fortunes bettered, he would reward them well. The fishermen readily consented, and being thus fully equipped, Pericles set off in his rusty armor to the King's Court.

In the tournament none bore himself so well as Pericles, and he won the wreath of victory, which the fair Princess herself placed on his brows. Then at her father's command she asked him who he was, and whence he came; and he answered that he was a knight of Tyre, by name Pericles, but he did not tell her that he was the King of that country, for he knew that if once his whereabouts became known to Antiochus, his life would not be worth a pin's purchase.

121

Nevertheless Thaisa loved him dearly, and the King was so pleased with his courage and graceful bearing that he gladly permitted his daughter to have her own way, when she told him she would marry the stranger knight or die.

Thus Pericles became the husband of the fair lady

PERICLES WINS IN THE TOURNAMENT.

for whose sake he had striven with the knights who came in all their bravery to joust and tourney for her love. Meanwhile the wicked King Antiochus had died, and the people in Tyre, hearing no news of their King, urged Lord Helicanus to ascend the vacant throne. But they could only get him to promise that he would become their King, if at the end of a year Pericles did not come back. Moreover, he sent forth messengers far and wide in search of the missing Pericles.

Some of these made their way to Pentapolis, and finding their King there, told him how discontented his people were at his long absence, and that, Antiochus being dead, there was nothing now to hinder him from returning to his kingdom. Then Pericles told his wife and father-in-law who he really was, and they and all the subjects of Simonides greatly rejoiced to know that the gallant husband of Thaisa was a King in his own right. So Pericles set sail with his dear wife for his native land. But once more the sea was cruel to him, for again a dreadful storm broke out, and while it was at its height, a servant came to tell him that a little daughter was born to him. This news would have made his heart glad indeed, but that the servant went on to add that his wife—his dear, dear Thaisa—was dead.

While he was praying the gods to be good to his little baby girl, the sailors came to him, declaring that the dead Queen must be thrown overboard, for they believed that the storm would never cease so

123

long as a dead body remained in the vessel. So
Thaisa was laid in a big chest with spices and jewels, and a scroll on which the sorrowful King wrote
these lines:—

"Here I give to understand
(If e'er this coffin drive a-land),
I, King Pericles, have lost
This Queen worth all our mundane cost.
Who finds her, give her burying;
She was the daughter of a King;
Besides this treasure for a fee,
The gods requite his charity!"

Then the chest was cast into the sea, and the
waves taking it, by and by washed it ashore at Ephesus, where it was found by the servants of a lord
named Cerimon. He at once ordered it to be
opened, and when he saw how lovely Thaisa looked,
he doubted if she were dead, and took immediate
steps to restore her. Then a great wonder happened, for she, who had been thrown into the sea
as dead, came back to life. But feeling sure that
she would never see her husband again, Thaisa retired from the world, and became a priestess of the
Goddess Diana.

124

While these things were happening, Pericles went on to Tarsus with his little daughter, whom he called Marina, because she had been born at sea. Leaving her in the hands of his old friend the Governor of Tarsus, the King sailed for his own dominions.

Now Dionyza, the wife of the Governor of Tarsus, was a jealous and wicked woman, and finding that the young Princess grew up a more accomplished and charming girl than her own daughter, she determined to take Marina's life. So when Marina was fourteen, Dionyza ordered one of her servants to take her away and kill her. This villain would have done so, but that he was interrupted by some pirates who came in and carried Marina off to sea with them, and took her to Mitylene, where they sold her as a slave. Yet such was her goodness, her grace, and her beauty, that she soon became honored there, and Lysimachus, the young Governor, fell deep in love with her, and would have married her, but that he thought she must be of too humble parentage to become the wife of one in his high position.

The wicked Dionyza believed, from her servant's

report, that Marina was really dead, and so she put up a monument to her memory, and showed it to King Pericles, when after long years of absence he came to see his much-loved child. When he heard that she was dead, his grief was terrible to see. He set sail once more, and putting on sackcloth, vowed never to wash his face or cut his hair again. There was a pavilion erected on deck, and there he lay alone, and for three months he spoke word to none.

At last it chanced that his ship came into the port of Mitylene, and Lysimachus, the Governor, went on board to enquire whence the vessel came. When he heard the story of Pericles' sorrow and silence, he bethought him of Marina, and believing that she could rouse the King from his stupor, sent for her and bade her try her utmost to persuade the King to speak, promising whatever reward she would, if she succeeded. Marina gladly obeyed, and sending the rest away, she sat and sang to her poor grief-laden father, yet, sweet as was her voice, he made no sign. So presently she spoke to him, saying that her grief might equal his, for, though she

126

was a slave, she came from ancestors that stood equal to mighty kings.

Something in her voice and story touched the King's heart, and he looked up at her, and as he looked, he saw with wonder how like she was to his

PERICLES AND MARINA.

lost wife, so with a great hope springing up in his heart, he bade her tell her story.

Then, with many interruptions from the King, she told him who she was and how she had escaped from the cruel Dionyza. So Pericles knew that this was indeed his daughter, and he kissed her again and again, crying that his great seas of joy drowned

127

him with their sweetness. "Give me my robes," he said: "O Heaven, bless my girl!"

Then there came to him, though none else could hear it, the sound of heavenly music, and falling asleep, he beheld the goddess Diana, in a vision.

"Go," she said to him, "to my temple at Ephesus, and when my maiden priests are met together, reveal how thou at sea didst lose thy wife."

Pericles obeyed the goddess and told his tale before her altar. Hardly had he made an end, when the chief priestess, crying out, "You are—you are— O royal Pericles!" fell fainting to the ground, and presently recovering, she spoke again to him, "O my lord, are you not Pericles?" "The voice of dead Thaisa!" exclaimed the King in wonder. "That Thaisa am I," she said, and looking at her he saw that she spoke the very truth.

Thus Pericles and Thaisa, after long and bitter suffering, found happiness once more, and in the joy of their meeting they forgot the pain of the past. To Marina great happiness was given, and not only in being restored to her dear parents; for she married Lysimachus, and became a princess in the land where she had been sold as a slave.

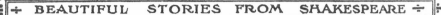

## HAMLET

HAMLET was the only son of the King of Denmark. He loved his father and mother dearly—and was happy in the love of a sweet lady named Ophelia. Her father, Polonius, was the King's Chamberlain.

While Hamlet was away studying at Wittenberg, his father died. Young Hamlet hastened home in great grief to hear that a serpent had stung the King, and that he was dead. The young Prince had loved his father so tenderly that you may judge what he felt when he found that the Queen, before yet the King had been laid in the ground a month, had determined to marry again—and to marry the dead King's brother.

Hamlet refused to put off mourning for the wedding.

"It is not only the black I wear on my body," he said, "that proves my loss. I wear mourning in my

129

heart for my dead father. His son at least re-members him, and grieves still."

Then said Claudius the King's brother, "This grief is unreasonable. Of course you must sorrow at the loss of your father, but—"

"Ah," said Hamlet, bitterly, "I cannot in one little month forget those I love."

With that the Queen and Claudius left him, to make merry over their wedding, forgetting the poor good King who had been so kind to them both.

And Hamlet, left alone, began to wonder and to question as to what he ought to do. For he could not believe the story about the snake-bite. It seemed to him all too plain that the wicked Claudius had killed the King, so as to get the crown and marry the Queen. Yet he had no proof, and could not accuse Claudius.

And while he was thus thinking came Horatio, a fellow student of his, from Wittenberg.

"What brought you here?" asked Hamlet, when he had greeted his friend kindly.

"I came, my lord, to see your father's funeral."

"I think it was to see my mother's wedding," said

Hamlet, bitterly. "My father! We shall not look upon his like again."

"My lord," answered Horatio, "I think I saw him yesternight."

Then, while Hamlet listened in surprise, Horatio told how he, with two gentlemen of the guard, had seen the King's ghost on the battlements. Hamlet went that night, and true enough, at midnight, the ghost of the King, in the armor he had been wont to wear, appeared on the battlements in

THE KING'S GHOST APPEARS.

the chill moonlight. Hamlet was a brave youth. Instead of running away from the ghost he spoke to it—and when it beckoned him he followed it to a quiet place, and there the ghost told him that what he had suspected was true. The wicked Claudius had indeed killed his good brother the King, by

131

dropping poison into his ear as he slept in his orchard in the afternoon.

"And you," said the ghost, "must avenge this cruel murder—on my wicked brother. But do nothing against the Queen—for I have loved her, and she is your mother. Remember me."

Then seeing the morning approach, the ghost vanished.

"Now," said Hamlet, "there is nothing left but revenge. Remember thee—I will remember nothing else—books, pleasure, youth—let all go—and your commands alone live on my brain."

So when his friends came back he made them swear to keep the secret of the ghost, and then went in from the battlements, now gray with mingled dawn and moonlight, to think how he might best avenge his murdered father.

The shock of seeing and hearing his father's ghost made him feel almost mad, and for fear that his uncle might notice that he was not himself, he determined to hide his mad longing for revenge under a pretended madness in other matters.

And when he met Ophelia, who loved him—and

132

to whom he had given gifts, and letters, and many
loving words—he behaved so wildly to her, that she
could not but think him mad.   For she loved him
so that she could not believe he would be as cruel as
this, unless he were quite mad.   So she told her
father, and showed him a pretty letter from Hamlet.
And in the letter was much folly, and this pretty
verse—

> " Doubt that the stars are fire;
>     Doubt that the sun doth move;
>  Doubt truth to be a liar;
>     But never doubt I love."

And from that time everyone believed that the cause
of Hamlet's supposed madness was love.

Poor Hamlet was very unhappy.   He longed to
obey his father's ghost—and yet he was too gentle
and kindly to wish to kill another man, even his
father's murderer.   And sometimes he wondered
whether, after all, the ghost spoke truly.

Just at this time some actors came to the Court,
and Hamlet ordered them to perform a certain play
before the King and Queen.   Now, this play was
the story of a man *who had been murdered in his*

*garden by a near relation, who afterwards married the dead man's wife.*

You may imagine the feelings of the wicked King, as he sat on his throne, with the Queen beside him and all his Court around, and saw, acted on the stage, the very wickedness that he had himself done. And when, in the play, the wicked relation poured poison into the ear of the sleeping man, the wicked Claudius suddenly rose, and staggered from the room—the Queen and others following.

Then said Hamlet to his friends—

"Now I am sure the ghost spoke true. For if Claudius had not done this murder, he could not have been so distressed to see it in a play."

Now the Queen sent for Hamlet, by the King's desire, to scold him for his conduct during the play, and for other matters; and Claudius, wishing to know exactly what happened, told old Polonius to hide himself behind the hangings in the Queen's room. And as they talked, the Queen got frightened at Hamlet's rough, strange words, and cried for help, and Polonius behind the curtain cried out too. Hamlet, thinking it was the King who was hidden there, thrust with his sword at the hangings, and killed, not the King, but poor old Polonius.

So now Hamlet had offended his uncle and his

POLONIUS KILLED BY HAMLET.

mother, and by bad hap killed his true love's father.

"Oh! what a rash and bloody deed is this," cried the Queen.

135

And Hamlet answered bitterly, "Almost as bad as to kill a king, and marry his brother." Then Hamlet told the Queen plainly all his thoughts and how he knew of the murder, and begged her, at least, to have no more friendship or kindness of the base Claudius, who had killed the good King. And as they spoke the King's ghost again appeared before Hamlet, but the Queen could not see it. So when the ghost had gone, they parted.

When the Queen told Claudius what had passed, and how Polonius was dead, he said, "This shows plainly that Hamlet is mad, and since he has killed the Chancellor, it is for his own safety that we must carry out our plan, and send him away to England."

So Hamlet was sent, under charge of two courtiers who served the King, and these bore letters to the English Court, requiring that Hamlet should be put to death. But Hamlet had the good sense to get at these letters, and put in others instead, with the names of the two courtiers who were so ready to betray him. Then, as the vessel went to England, Hamlet escaped on board a pirate ship, and the two wicked courtiers left him to his fate, and went on to meet theirs.

Hamlet hurried home, but in the meantime a dreadful thing had happened. Poor pretty Ophelia, having lost her lover and her father, lost her wits too, and went in sad madness about the Court, with straws, and weeds, and flowers in her hair, singing strange scraps of songs, and talking poor, foolish, pretty talk with no heart of meaning to it. And one day, coming to a stream where willows grew, she tried to hang a flowery garland on a willow, and fell into the water with all her flowers, and so died.

DROWNING OF OPHELIA.

And Hamlet had loved her, though his plan of seeming madness had made him hide it; and when

137

he came back, he found the King and Queen, and the Court, weeping at the funeral of his dear love and lady.

Ophelia's brother, Laertes, had also just come to Court to ask justice for the death of his father, old Polonius; and now, wild with grief, he leaped into his sister's grave, to clasp her in his arms once more.

"I loved her more than forty thousand brothers," cried Hamlet, and leapt into the grave after him, and they fought till they were parted.

Afterwards Hamlet begged Laertes to forgive him.

"I could not bear," he said, "that any, even a brother, should seem to love her more than I."

But the wicked Claudius would not let them be friends.  He told Laertes how Hamlet had killed old Polonius, and between them they made a plot to slay Hamlet by treachery.

Laertes challenged him to a fencing match, and all the Court were present.  Hamlet had the blunt foil always used in fencing, but Laertes had prepared for himself a sword, sharp, and tipped with poison.  And the wicked King had made ready a bowl of poisoned wine, which he meant to give poor Hamlet when he should grow warm with the sword play, and should call for drink.

So Laertes and Hamlet fought, and Laertes, after some fencing, gave Hamlet a sharp sword thrust. Hamlet, angry at this treachery—for they had been fencing, not as men fight, but as they play —closed with Laertes in a struggle; both dropped their swords, and when they picked them up again, Hamlet, without noticing it, had exchanged his own blunt sword for Laertes' sharp and poisoned one. And with one thrust of it he pierced Laertes, who fell dead by his own treachery.

At this moment the Queen cried out, "The drink, the drink! Oh, my dear Hamlet! I am poisoned!"

She had drunk of the poisoned bowl the King had prepared for Hamlet, and the King saw the Queen, whom, wicked as he was, he really loved, fall dead by his means.

Then Ophelia being dead, and Polonius, and the Queen, and Laertes, and the two courtiers who had been sent to England, Hamlet at last found courage to do the ghost's bidding and avenge his father's

139

murder—which, if he had braced up his heart to do long before, all these lives had been spared, and none had suffered but the wicked King, who well deserved to die.

Hamlet, his heart at last being great enough to do the deed he ought, turned the poisoned sword on the false King.

"Then—venom—do thy work!" he cried, and the King died.

So Hamlet in the end kept the promise he had made his father. And all being now accomplished, he himself died. And those who stood by saw him die, with prayers and tears, for his friends and his people loved him with their whole hearts. Thus ends the tragic tale of Hamlet, Prince of Denmark.

IACHIMO AND IMOGEN.

## CYMBELINE

CYMBELINE was the King of Britain. He had three children. The two sons were stolen away from him when they were quite little children, and he was left with only one daughter, Imogen. The King married a second time, and brought up Leonatus, the son of a dear friend, as Imogen's playfellow; and when Leonatus was old enough, Imogen secretly married him. This made the King and Queen very angry, and the King, to punish Leonatus, banished him from Britain.

141

Poor Imogen was nearly heart-broken at parting from Leonatus, and he was not less unhappy. For they were not only lovers and husband and wife, but they had been friends and comrades ever since they were quite little children. With many tears and kisses they said "Good-bye." They promised never to forget each other, and that they would never care for anyone else as long as they lived.

"This diamond was my mother's, love," said Imogen; "take it, my heart, and keep it as long as you love me."

"Sweetest, fairest," answered Leonatus, "wear this bracelet for my sake."

"Ah!" cried Imogen, weeping, "when shall we meet again?"

And while they were still in each other's arms, the King came in, and Leonatus had to leave without more farewell.

When he was come to Rome, where he had gone to stay with an old friend of his father's, he spent his days still in thinking of his dear Imogen, and his nights in dreaming of her. One day at a feast some Italian and French noblemen were talking of their sweethearts, and swearing that they were the most faithful and honorable and beautiful ladies in the world. And a Frenchman reminded Leonatus how he had said many times that his wife Imogen was more fair, wise, and constant than any of the ladies in France.

"I say so still," said Leonatus.

"She is not so good but that she would deceive," said Iachimo, one of the Italian nobles.

"She never would deceive," said Leonatus.

"I wager," said Iachimo, "that, if I go to Britain, I can persuade your wife to do whatever I wish, even if it should be against your wishes."

"That you will never do," said Leonatus. "I wager this ring upon my finger," which was the very ring Imogen had given him at parting, "that my wife will keep all her vows to me, and that you will never persuade her to do otherwise."

So Iachimo wagered half his estate against the ring on Leonatus's finger, and started forthwith for Britain, with a letter of introduction to Leonatus's wife. When he reached there he was received with all kindness; but he was still determined to win his wager.

He told Imogen that her husband thought no more of her, and went on to tell many cruel lies about him. Imogen listened at first, but presently perceived what a wicked person Iachimo was, and ordered him to leave her. Then he said—

"Pardon me, fair lady, all that I have said is untrue. I only told you this to see whether you would believe me, or whether you were as much to be trusted as your husband thinks. Will you forgive me?"

"I forgive you freely," said Imogen.

"Then," went on Iachimo, "perhaps you will prove it by taking charge of a trunk, containing a number of jewels which your husband and I and some other gentlemen have bought as a present for the Emperor of Rome."

"I will indeed," said Imogen, "do anything for my husband and a friend of my husband's. Have the jewels sent into my room, and I will take care of them."

"It is only for one night," said Iachimo, "for I leave Britain again to-morrow."

So the trunk was carried into Imogen's room, and

that night she went to bed and to sleep. When she was fast asleep, the lid of the trunk opened and a man got out. It was Iachimo. The story about the jewels was as untrue as the rest of the things he had said. He had only wished to get into her room to win his wicked wager. He looked about him and noticed the fur-niture, and then crept to the side of the bed where Imogen was asleep and took

IACHIMO IN THE TRUNK.

from her arm the gold bracelet which had been the parting gift of her husband. Then he crept back to the trunk, and next morning sailed for Rome.

When he met Leonatus, he said—

"I have been to Britain and I have won the wager, for your wife no longer thinks about you. She stayed talking with me all one night in her room, which is hung with tapestry and has a carved chim-ney-piece, and silver andirons in the shape of two winking Cupids."

" I do not believe she has forgotten me; I do not

145

believe she stayed talking with you in her room. You have heard her room described by the servants."

"Ah!" said Iachimo, "but she gave me this brace-let. She took it from her arm. I see her yet. Her pretty action did outsell her gift, and yet enriched it too. She gave it me, and said she prized it once."

"Take the ring," cried Leonatus, "you have won; and you might have won my life as well, for I care nothing for it now I know my lady has forgotten me."

And mad with anger, he wrote letters to Britain to his old servant, Pisanio, ordering him to take Imo-gen to Milford Haven, and to murder her, because she had forgotten him and given away his gift. At the same time he wrote to Imogen herself, telling her to go with Pisanio, his old servant, to Milford Haven, and that he, her husband, would be there to meet her.

Now when Pisanio got this letter he was too good to carry out its orders, and too wise to let them alone altogether. So he gave Imogen the letter from her husband, and started with her for Milford Haven. Before he left, the wicked Queen gave him a drink which, she said, would be useful in sickness. She hoped he would give it to Imogen, and that Imogen would die, and the wicked Queen's son could be King. For the Queen thought this drink was a poison, but really and truly it was only a sleeping-draft.

When Pisanio and Imogen came near to Milford Haven, he told her what was really in the letter he had had from her husband.

"I must go on to Rome, and see him myself," said Imogen.

And then Pisanio helped her to dress in boy's clothes, and sent her on her way, and went back to the Court. Before he went he gave her the drink he had had from the Queen.

Imogen went on, getting more and more tired, and at last came to a cave. Someone seemed to live there, but no one was in just then. So she went in, and as she was almost dying of hunger, she took some food she saw there, and had just done so, when an old man and two boys came into the cave. She was very much frightened when she saw them, for she thought that they would be angry with her for taking their food, though she had meant to leave money for it on the table. But to her surprise they welcomed her kindly. She looked very pretty in her boy's clothes and her face was good, as well as pretty.

"You shall be our brother," said both the boys; and so she stayed with them, and helped to cook the food, and make things comfortable. But one day when the old man, whose name was Bellarius, was out hunting with the two boys, Imogen felt ill, and thought she would try the medicine Pisanio had given her. So she took it, and at once became like a dead creature, so that when Bellarius and the boys came back from hunting, they thought she was dead, and with many tears and funeral songs, they carried her away and laid her in the wood, covered with flowers.

They sang sweet songs to her, and strewed flowers on her, pale primroses, and the azure harebell, and eglantine, and furred moss, and went away sorrowful. No sooner had they gone than Imogen awoke, and not knowing how she came there, nor where she was, went wandering through the wood.

Now while Imogen had been living in the cave, the Romans had decided to attack Britain, and their army had come over, and with them Leonatus, who had grown sorry for his wickedness against Imogen, so had come back, not to fight with the Romans against Britain, but with the Britons against Rome. So as Imogen wandered alone, she met with Lucius, the Roman General, and took service with him as his page.

When the battle was fought between the Romans and Britons, Bellarius and his two boys fought for their own country, and Leonatus, disguised as a British peasant, fought beside them. The Romans had taken Cymbeline prisoner, and old Bellarius, with his sons and Leonatus, bravely rescued the King. Then the Britons won the battle, and among the prisoners brought before the King were Lucius, with Imogen, Iachimo, and Leonatus, who had put on the uniform of a Roman soldier. He was tired of his life since he had cruelly ordered his wife to be killed, and he hoped that, as a Roman soldier, he would be put to death.

When they were brought before the King, Lucius spoke out—

149

"A Roman with a Roman's heart can suffer," he said. "If I must die, so be it. This one thing only will I entreat. My boy, a Briton born, let him be ransomed. Never master had a page so kind, so duteous, diligent, true. He has done no Briton harm, though he has served a Roman. Save him, sir."

Then Cymbeline looked on the page, who was his

IMOGEN STUPEFIED.

own daughter, Imogen, in disguise, and though he did not recognize her, he felt such a kindness that he not only spared the boy's life, but he said—

"He shall have any boon he likes to ask of me, even though he ask a prisoner, the noblest taken."

Then Imogen said, "The boon I ask is that this gentleman shall say from whom he got the ring he has on his finger," and she pointed to Iachimo.

"Speak," said Cymbeline, "how did you get that diamond?"

Then Iachimo told the whole truth of his villainy. At this, Leonatus was unable to contain himself, and casting aside all thought of disguise, he came forward, cursing himself for his folly in having believed Iachimo's lying story, and calling again and again on his wife whom he believed dead.

IMOGEN AND LEONATUS.

"Oh, Imogen, my love, my life!" he cried. "Oh, Imogen!"

Then Imogen, forgetting she was disguised, cried out, "Peace, my lord—here, here!"

151

Leonatus turned to strike the forward page who thus interfered in his great trouble, and then he saw that it was his wife, Imogen, and they fell into each other's arms.

The King was so glad to see his dear daughter again, and so grateful to the man who had rescued him (whom he now found to be Leonatus), that he gave his blessing on their marriage, and then he turned to Bellarius, and the two boys. Now Bellarius spoke—

"I am your old servant, Bellarius. You accused me of treason when I had only been loyal to you, and to be doubted, made me disloyal. So I stole your two sons, and see,—they are here!" And he brought forward the two boys, who had sworn to be brothers to Imogen when they thought she was a boy like themselves.

The wicked Queen was dead of some of her own poisons, and the King, with his three children about him, lived to a happy old age.

So the wicked were punished, and the good and true lived happy ever after. So may the wicked suffer, and honest folk prosper till the world's end.

THE THREE WITCHES.

## MACBETH

WHEN a person is asked to tell the story of Macbeth, he can tell two stories. One is of a man called Macbeth who came to the throne of Scotland by a crime in the year of our Lord 1039, and reigned justly and well, on the whole, for fifteen years or more. This story is part of Scottish history. The other story issues from a place called Imagination; it is gloomy and wonderful, and you shall hear it.

**153**

A year or two before Edward the Confessor began to rule England, a battle was won in Scotland against a Norwegian King by two generals named Macbeth and Banquo. After the battle, the generals walked together towards Forres, in Elginshire, where Duncan, King of Scotland, was awaiting them.

FROM "MACBETH."

While they were crossing a lonely heath, they saw three bearded women, sisters, hand in hand, withered in appearance and wild in their attire.

"Speak, who are you?" demanded Macbeth.

"Hail, Macbeth, chieftain of Glamis," said the first woman.

154

"Hail, Macbeth, chieftain of Cawdor," said the second woman.

"Hail, Macbeth, King that is to be," said the third woman.

Then Banquo asked, "What of me?" and the third woman replied, "Thou shalt be the father of kings."

"Tell me more," said Macbeth. "By my father's death I am chieftain of Glamis, but the chieftain of Cawdor lives, and the King lives, and his children live. Speak, I charge you!"

The women replied only by vanishing, as though suddenly mixed with the air.

Banquo and Macbeth knew then that they had been addressed by witches, and were discussing their prophecies when two nobles approached. One of them thanked Macbeth, in the King's name, for his military services, and the other said, "He bade me call you chieftain of Cawdor."

Macbeth then learned that the man who had yesterday borne that title was to die for treason, and he could not help thinking, "The third witch called me, 'King that is to be.'"

"Banquo," he said, "you see that the witches spoke

truth concerning me. Do you not believe, therefore, that your child and grandchild will be kings?"

Banquo frowned. Duncan had two sons, Malcolm and Donalbain, and he deemed it disloyal to hope that his son Fleance should rule Scotland. He told Macbeth that the witches might have intended to tempt them both into villainy by their prophecies concerning the throne. Macbeth, however, thought the prophecy that he should be King too pleasant to keep to himself, and he mentioned it to his wife in a letter.

Lady Macbeth was the grand-daughter of a King of Scotland who had died in defending his crown against the King who preceded Duncan, and by whose order her only brother was slain. To her, Duncan was a reminder of bitter wrongs. Her husband had royal blood in his veins, and when she read his letter, she was determined that he should be King.

When a messenger arrived to inform her that Duncan would pass a night in Macbeth's castle, she nerved herself for a very base action.

She told Macbeth almost as soon as she saw him

that Duncan must spend a sunless morrow. She meant that Duncan must die, and that the dead are blind. "We will speak further," said Macbeth uneasily, and at night, with his memory full of Duncan's kind words, he would fain have spared his guest.

"Would you live a coward?" demanded Lady Macbeth, who seems to have thought that morality and cowardice were the same.

LADY MACBETH.

"I dare do all that may become a man," replied Macbeth; "who dare do more is none."

"Why did you write that letter to me?" she inquired fiercely, and with bitter words she egged him on to murder, and with cunning words she showed him how to do it.

After supper Duncan went to bed, and two grooms were placed on guard at his bedroom door. Lady Macbeth caused them to drink wine till they were stupefied. She then took their daggers and would have killed the King herself if his sleeping face had not looked like her father's.

Macbeth came later, and found the daggers lying by the grooms; and soon with red hands he appeared before his wife, saying, "Methought I heard a voice cry, 'Sleep no more! Macbeth destroys the sleep-ing.'"

"Wash your hands," said she. "Why did you not leave the daggers by the grooms? Take them back, and smear the grooms with blood."

"I dare not," said Macbeth.

His wife dared, and she returned to him with hands red as his own, but a heart less white, she proudly told him, for she scorned his fear.

The murderers heard a knocking, and Macbeth wished it was a knocking which could wake the dead. It was the knocking of Macduff, the chieftain of

Fife, who had been told by Duncan to visit him early. Macbeth went to him, and showed him the door of the King's room.

Macduff entered, and came out again crying, "O horror! horror! horror!"

Macbeth appeared as horror-stricken as Macduff, and pretending that he could not bear to see life in

KING AND QUEEN MACBETH.

Duncan's murderers, he slew the two grooms with their own daggers before they could proclaim their innocence.

These murders did not shriek out, and Macbeth was crowned at Scone. One of Duncan's sons went to Ireland, the other to England. Macbeth was

King. But he was discontented. The prophecy concerning Banquo oppressed his mind. If Fleance were to rule, a son of Macbeth would not rule. Macbeth determined, therefore, to murder both Banquo and his son. He hired two ruffians, who slew Banquo one night when he was on his way with Fleance to a banquet which Macbeth was giving to his nobles. Fleance escaped.

Meanwhile Macbeth and his Queen received their guests very graciously, and he expressed a wish for them which has been uttered thousands of times since his day—"Now good digestion wait on appetite, and health on both."

"We pray your Majesty to sit with us," said Lennox, a Scotch noble; but ere Macbeth could reply, the ghost of Banquo entered the banqueting hall and sat in Macbeth's place.

Not noticing the ghost, Macbeth observed that, if Banquo were present, he could say that he had collected under his roof the choicest chivalry of Scotland. Macduff, however, had curtly declined his invitation.

The King was again pressed to take a seat, and

160

Lennox, to whom Banquo's ghost was invisible, showed him the chair where it sat.

But Macbeth, with his eyes of genius, saw the ghost. He saw it like a form of mist and blood, and he demanded passionately, "Which of you have done this?"

Still none saw the ghost but he, and to the ghost Macbeth said, "Thou canst not say I did it."

The ghost glided out, and Macbeth was impudent enough to raise a glass of wine "to the general joy of the whole table, and to our dear friend Banquo, whom we miss."

The toast was drunk as the ghost of Banquo entered for the second time.

"Begone!" cried Macbeth. "You are senseless, mindless! Hide in the earth, thou horrible shadow."

Again none saw the ghost but he.

"What is it your Majesty sees?" asked one of the nobles.

The Queen dared not permit an answer to be given to this question. She hurriedly begged her guests to quit a sick man who was likely to grow worse if he was obliged to talk.

Macbeth, however, was well enough next day to converse with the witches whose prophecies had so depraved him.

He found them in a cavern on a thunderous day. They were revolving round a cauldron in which were boiling particles of many strange and horrible creatures, and they knew he was coming before he arrived.

"Answer me what I ask you," said the King.

"Would you rather hear it from us or our masters?" asked the first witch.

"Call them," replied Macbeth.

Thereupon the witches poured blood into the cauldron and grease into the flame that licked it, and a helmeted head appeared with the visor on, so that Macbeth could only see its eyes.

He was speaking to the head, when the first witch said gravely, "He knows thy thought," and a voice in the head said, "Macbeth, beware Macduff, the chieftain of Fife." The head then descended into the cauldron till it disappeared.

"One word more," pleaded Macbeth.

"He will not be commanded," said the first witch,

162

and then a crowned child ascended from the cauldron bearing a tree in his hand. The child said—

> " Macbeth shall be unconquerable till
>     The Wood of Birnam climbs Dunsinane Hill."

"That will never be," said Macbeth; and he asked
to be told if Banquo's descendants would ever rule
Scotland.

The cauldron sank into the earth; music was
heard, and a procession of phantom kings filed past
Macbeth; behind them was Banquo's ghost. In
each king Macbeth saw a likeness to Banquo, and he
counted eight kings.

Then he was suddenly left alone.

His next proceeding was to send murderers to
Macduff's castle. They did not find Macduff, and
asked Lady Macduff where he was. She gave a
stinging answer, and her questioner called Macduff
a traitor. "Thou liest!" shouted Macduff's little
son, who was immediately stabbed, and with his last
breath entreated his mother to fly. The murderers
did not leave the castle while one of its inmates remained alive.

Macduff was in England listening, with Malcolm, to a doctor's tale of cures wrought by Edward the Confessor when his friend Ross came to tell him that his wife and children were no more. At first Ross dared not speak the truth, and turn Macduff's bright sympathy with sufferers relieved by royal virtue into sorrow and hatred. But when Malcolm said that England was sending an army into Scotland against Macbeth, Ross blurted out his news, and Macduff cried, *"All* dead, did you say? *All* my pretty ones and their mother? Did you say *all?"*

His sorry hope was in revenge, but if he could have looked into Macbeth's castle on Dunsinane Hill, he would have seen at work a force more solemn than revenge. Retribution was working, for Lady Macbeth was mad. She walked in her sleep amid ghastly dreams. She was wont to wash her hands for a quarter of an hour at a time; but after all her washing, would still see a red spot of blood upon her skin. It was pitiful to hear her cry that all the perfumes of Arabia could not sweeten her little hand.

"Canst thou not minister to a mind diseased?"

inquired Macbeth of the doctor, but the doctor replied that his patient must minister to her own mind. This reply gave Macbeth a scorn of medicine. "Throw physic to the dogs," he said; "I'll none of it."

One day he heard a sound of women crying. An officer approched him and said, "The Queen, your Majesty, is dead." "Out, brief candle," muttered Macbeth, meaning that life was like a candle, at the mercy of a puff of air. He did not weep; he was too familiar with death.

Presently a messenger told him that he saw Birnam Wood on the march. Macbeth called him a liar and a slave, and threatened to hang him if he had made a mistake. "If you are right you can hang me," he said.

From the turret windows of Dunsinane Castle, Birnam Wood did indeed appear to be marching. Every soldier of the English army held aloft a bough which he had cut from a tree in that wood, and like human trees they climbed Dunsinane Hill.

Macbeth had still his courage. He went to battle to conquer or die, and the first thing he did was to

kill the English general's son in single combat.
Macbeth then felt that no man could fight him and
live, and when Macduff came to him blazing for
revenge, Macbeth said to him, "Go back; I have
spilt too much of your blood already."

MACBETH AND MACDUFF FIGHT.

"My voice is in my sword," replied Macduff,
and hacked at him and bade him yield.

"I will not yield!" said Macbeth, but his last hour
had struck. He fell.

Macbeth's men were in retreat when Macduff

166

came before Malcolm holding a King's head by the hair.

"Hail, King!" he said; and the new King looked at the old.

So Malcolm reigned after Macbeth; but in years that came afterwards the descendants of Banquo were kings.

## THE COMEDY OF ERRORS

ÆGEON was a merchant of Syracuse, which is a seaport in Sicily. His wife was Æmilia, and they were very happy until Ægeon's manager died, and he was obliged to go by himself to a place called Epidamnum on the Adriatic. As soon as she could Æmilia followed him, and after they had been together some time two baby boys were born to them. The babies were exactly alike; even when they were dressed differently they looked the same.

And now you must believe a very strange thing. At the same inn where these children were born, and on the same day, two baby boys were born to a much poorer couple than Æmilia and Ægeon; so poor, indeed, were the parents of these twins that they sold them to the parents of the other twins.

Æmilia was eager to show her children to her friends in Syracuse, and in treacherous weather she and Ægeon and the four babies sailed homewards.

168

They were still far from Syracuse when their ship sprang a leak, and the crew left it in a body by the only boat, caring little what became of their passengers.

Æmilia fastened one of her children to a mast and tied one of the slave-children to him; Ægeon followed her example with the remaining children. Then the parents secured themselves to the same masts, and hoped for safety.

The ship, however, suddenly struck a rock and was split in two, and Æmilia, and the two children whom she had tied, floated away from Ægeon and the other children. Æmilia and her charges were picked up by some people of Epidamnum, but some fishermen of Corinth took the babies from her by force, and she returned to Epidamnum alone, and very miserable. Afterwards she settled in Ephesus, a famous town in Asia Minor.

Ægeon and his charges were also saved; and, more fortunate than Æmilia, he was able to return to Syracuse and keep them till they were eighteen. His own child he called Antipholus, and the slave-child he called Dromio; and, strangely enough, these

169

were the names given to the children who floated away from him.

At the age of eighteen the son who was with Ægeon grew restless with a desire to find his brother. Ægeon let him depart with his servant, and the

ANTIPHOLUS AND DROMIO.

young men are henceforth known as Antipholus of Syracuse and Dromio of Syracuse.

Let alone, Ægeon found his home too dreary to dwell in, and traveled for five years. He did not, during his absence, learn all the news of Syracuse, or he would never have gone to Ephesus.

As it was, his melancholy wandering ceased in that town, where he was arrested almost as soon as he arrived. He then found that the Duke of Syracuse had been acting in so tyrannical a manner to Ephesians unlucky enough to fall into his hands, that the Government of Ephesus had angrily passed a law which punished by death or a fine of a thousand pounds any Syracusan who should come to Ephesus. Ægeon was brought before Solinus, Duke of Ephesus, who told him that he must die or pay a thousand pounds before the end of the day.

You will think there was fate in this when I tell you that the children who were kidnaped by the fishermen of Corinth were now citizens of Ephesus, whither they had been brought by Duke Menaphon, an uncle of Duke Solinus. They will henceforth be called Antipholus of Ephesus and Dromio of Ephesus.

Moreover, on the very day when Ægeon was arrested, Antipholus of Syracuse landed in Ephesus and pretended that he came from Epidamnum in order to avoid a penalty. He handed his money to his servant Dromio of Syracuse, and bade him take it to the Centaur Inn and remain there till he came.

In less than ten minutes he was met on the Mart by Dromio of Ephesus, his brother's slave, and immediately mistook him for his own Dromio. "Why are you back so soon? Where did you leave the money?" asked Antipholus of Syracuse.

This Dromio knew of no money except sixpence, which he had received on the previous Wednesday and given to the saddler; but he did know that his mistress was annoyed because his master was not in to dinner, and he asked Antipholus of Syracuse to go to a house called The Phœnix without delay. His speech angered the hearer, who would have beaten him if he had not fled. Antipholus of Syracuse them went to The Centaur, found that his gold had been deposited there, and walked out of the inn.

He was wandering about Ephesus when two beautiful ladies signaled to him with their hands. They were sisters, and their names were Adriana and Luciana. Adriana was the wife of his brother Antipholus of Ephesus, and she had made up her mind, from the strange account given her by Dromio

172

of Ephesus, that her husband preferred another woman to his wife. "Ay, you may look as if you did not know me," she said to the man who was really her brother-in-law, "but I can remember when no words were sweet unless I said them, no meat flavorsome unless I carved it."

"Is it I you address?" said Antipholus of Syracuse stiffly. "I do not know you."

"Fie, brother," said Luciana. "You know perfectly well that she sent Dromio to you to bid you come to dinner"; and Adriana said, "Come, come; I have been made a fool of long enough. My truant husband shall dine with me and confess his silly pranks and be forgiven."

They were determined ladies, and Antipholus of Syracuse grew weary of disputing with them, and followed them obediently to The Phœnix, where a very late "mid-day" dinner awaited them.

They were at dinner when Antipholus of Ephesus and his slave Dromio demanded admittance. "Maud, Bridget, Marian, Cecily, Gillian, Ginn!" shouted Dromio of Ephesus, who knew all his fellow-servants' names by heart.

From within came the reply, "Fool, dray-horse, coxcomb, idiot!" It was Dromio of Syracuse unconsciously insulting his brother.

Master and man did their best to get in, short of using a crowbar, and finally went away; but Antipholus of Ephesus felt so annoyed with his wife that he decided to give a gold chain which he had promised her, to another woman.

Inside The Phœnix, Luciana, who believed Antipholus of Syracuse to be her sister's husband, attempted, by a discourse in rhyme, when alone with him, to make him kinder to Adriana. In reply he told her that he was not married, but that he loved her so much that, if Luciana were a mermaid, he would gladly lie on the sea if he might feel beneath him her floating golden hair.

Luciana was shocked and left him, and reported his lovemaking to Adriana, who said that her husband was old and ugly, and not fit to be seen or heard, though secretly she was very fond of him.

Antipholus of Syracuse soon received a visitor in the shape of Angelo the goldsmith, of whom Antipholus of Ephesus had ordered the chain which he

174

had promised his wife and intended to give to another woman.

The goldsmith handed the chain to Antipholus of Syracuse, and treated his "I bespoke it not" as mere fun, so that the puzzled merchant took the chain as

LUCIANA AND ANTIPHOLUS OF SYRACUSE.

good-humoredly as he had partaken of Adriana's dinner. He offered payment, but Angelo foolishly said he would call again.

The consequence was that Angelo was without money when a creditor of the sort that stands no nonsense, threatened him with arrest unless he paid

175

his debt immediately. This creditor had brought a police officer with him, and Angelo was relieved to see Antipholus of Ephesus coming out of the house where he had been dining because he had been locked out of The Phœnix. Bitter was Angelo's dismay when Antipholus denied receipt of the chain. Angelo could have sent his mother to prison if she had said that, and he gave Antipholus of Ephesus in charge.

At this moment up came Dromio of Syracuse and told the wrong Antipholus that he had shipped his goods, and that a favorable wind was blowing. To the ears of Antipholus of Ephesus this talk was simple nonsense. He would gladly have beaten the slave, but contented himself with crossly telling him to hurry to Adriana and bid her send to her arrested husband a purse of money which she would find in his desk.

Though Adriana was furious with her husband because she thought he had been making love to her sister, she did not prevent Luciana from getting the purse, and she bade Dromio of Syracuse bring home his master immediately.

Unfortunately, before Dromio could reach the police station he met his real master, who had never been arrested, and did not understand what he meant by offering him a purse. Antipholus of Syracuse was further surprised when a lady whom he did not know asked him for a chain that he had promised her. She was, of course, the lady with whom Antipholus of Ephesus had dined when his brother was occupying his place at table. "Avaunt, thou witch!" was the answer which, to her astonishment, she received.

Meanwhile Antipholus of Ephesus waited vainly for the money which was to have released him. Never a good-tempered man, he was crazy with anger when Dromio of Ephesus, who, of course, had not been instructed to fetch a purse, appeared with nothing more useful than a rope. He beat the slave in the street despite the remonstrance of the police officer; and his temper did not mend when Adriana, Luciana, and a doctor arrived under the impression that he was mad and must have his pulse felt. He raged so much that men came forward to bind him. But the kindness of Adriana spared him

177

this shame. She promised to pay the sum demanded of him, and asked the doctor to lead him to
The Phœnix.

Angelo's merchant creditor being paid, the two
were friendly again, and might soon have been seen
chatting before an abbey about the odd behavior

THE GOLDSMITH AND ANTIPHOLUS OF SYRACUSE.

of Antipholus of Ephesus. "Softly," said the merchant at last, "that's he, I think."

It was not; it was Antipholus of Syracuse with
his servant Dromio, and he wore Angelo's chain
round his neck! The reconciled pair fairly pounced
upon him to know what he meant by denying the

178

receipt of the chain he had the impudence to wear. Antipholus of Syracuse lost his temper, and drew his sword, and at that moment Adriana and several others appeared. "Hold!" shouted the careful wife. "Hurt him not; he is mad. Take his sword away. Bind him—and Dromio too."

Dromio of Syracuse did not wish to be bound, and he said to his master, "Run, master! Into that abbey, quick, or we shall be robbed!"

They accordingly retreated into the abbey.

Adriana, Luciana, and a crowd remained outside, and the Abbess came out, and said, "People, why do you gather here?"

"To fetch my poor distracted husband," replied Adriana.

Angelo and the merchant remarked that they had not known that he was mad.

Adriana then told the Abbess rather too much about her wifely worries, for the Abbess received the idea that Adriana was a shrew, and that if her husband was distracted he had better not return to her for the present.

Adriana determined, therefore, to complain to

179

Duke Solinus, and, lo and behold! a minute afterwards the great man appeared with officers and two others. The others were Ægeon and the headsman. The thousand marks had not been found, and Ægeon's fate seemed sealed.

Ere the Duke could pass the abbey Adriana knelt before him, and told a woeful tale of a mad husband rushing about stealing jewelry and drawing his sword, adding that the Abbess refused to allow her to lead him home.

The Duke bade the Abbess be summoned, and no sooner had he given the order than a servant from The Phœnix ran to Adriana with the tale that his master had singed off the doctor's beard.

"Nonsense!" said Adriana, "he's in the abbey."

"As sure as I live I speak the truth," said the servant.

Antipholus of Syracuse had not come out of the abbey, before his brother of Ephesus prostrated himself in front of the Duke, exclaiming, "Justice, most gracious Duke, against that woman." He pointed to Adriana. "She has treated another man like her husband in my own house."

180

Even while he was speaking Ægeon said, "Unless I am delirious, I see my son Antipholus."

No one noticed him, and A tipholus of Ephesus went on to say how the doctor, whom he called "a threadbare juggler," had been one of a gang who tied him to his slave Dromio, and thrust them into a vault whence he had escaped by gnawing through his bonds.

ÆMILIA.

The Duke could not understand how the same man who spoke to him was seen to go into the abbey, and he was still wondering when Ægeon asked Antipholus of Ephesus if he was not his son.  He

181

replied, "I never saw my father in my life;" but so deceived was Ægeon by his likeness to the brother whom he had brought up, that he said, "Thou art ashamed to acknowledge me in misery."

Soon, however, the Abbess advanced with Antipholus of Syracuse and Dromio of Syracuse.

Then cried Adriana, "I see two husbands or mine eyes deceive me;" and Antipholus, espying his father, said, "Thou art Ægeon or his ghost."

It was a day of surprises, for the Abbess said, "I will free that man by paying his fine, and gain my husband whom I lost. Speak, Ægeon, for I am thy wife Æmilia."

The Duke was touched. "He is free without a fine," he said.

So Ægeon and Æmilia were reunited, and Adriana and her husband reconciled; but no one was happier than Antipholus of Syracuse, who, in the Duke's presence, went to Luciana and said, "I told you I loved you. Will you be my wife?"

Her answer was given by a look, and therefore is not written.

The two Dromios were glad to think they would receive no more beatings.

## THE MERCHANT OF VENICE

ANTONIO was a rich and prosperous merchant of Venice. His ships were on nearly every sea, and he traded with Portugal, with Mexico, with England, and with India. Although proud of his riches, he was very generous with them, and delighted to use them in relieving the wants of his friends, among whom his relation, Bassanio, held the first place.

Now Bassanio, like many another gay and gallant gentleman, was reckless and extravagant, and finding that he had not only come to the end of his fortune, but was also unable to pay his creditors, he went to Antonio for further help.

"To you, Antonio," he said, "I owe the most in money and in love: and I have thought of a plan to pay everything I owe if you will but help me."

"Say what I can do, and it shall be done," answered his friend.

183

Then said Bassanio, "In Belmont is a lady richly left, and from all quarters of the globe renowned suitors come to woo her, not only because she is rich, but because she is beautiful and good as well. She looked on me with such favor when last we met, that I feel sure that I should win her away from all rivals for her love had I but the means to go to Belmont, where she lives."

"All my fortunes," said Antonio, "are at sea, and so I have no ready money; but luckily my credit is good in Venice, and I will borrow for you what you need."

There was living in Venice at this time a rich money-lender, named Shylock. Antonio despised and disliked this man very much, and treated him with the greatest harshness and scorn. He would thrust him, like a cur, over his threshold, and would even spit on him. Shylock submitted to all these indignities with a patient shrug; but deep in his heart he cherished a desire for revenge on the rich, smug merchant. For Antonio both hurt his pride and injured his business. "But for him," thought Shylock, "I should be richer by half a million

184

ducats. On the market place, and wherever he can, he denounces the rate of interest I charge, and— worse than that—he lends out money freely."

So when Bassanio came to him to ask for a loan of three thousand ducats to Antonio for three months, Shylock hid his hatred, and turning to Antonio, said—"Harshly as you have treated me, I would be friends with you and have your love. So I will lend you the money and charge you no interest. But, just for fun, you shall sign a bond in which it shall be agreed that if you do not repay me in three months' time, then I shall have the right to a pound of your flesh, to be cut from what part of your body I choose."

"No," cried Bassanio to his friend, "you shall run no such risk for me."

"Why, fear not," said Antonio, "my ships will be home a month before the time. I will sign the bond."

Thus Bassanio was furnished with the means to go to Belmont, there to woo the lovely Portia. The very night he started, the money-lender's pretty daughter, Jessica, ran away from her father's house

185

with her lover, and she took with her from her father's hoards some bags of ducats and precious stones. Shylock's grief and anger were terrible to see. His love for her changed to hate. "I would she were dead at my feet and the jewels in her ear," he cried. His only comfort now was in hearing of the serious losses which had befallen Antonio, some of whose ships were wrecked. "Let him look to his bond," said Shylock, "let him look to his bond."

Meanwhile Bassanio had reached Belmont, and had visited the fair Portia. He found, as he had told Antonio, that the rumor of her wealth and beauty had drawn to her suitors from far and near. But to all of them Portia had but one reply. She would only accept that suitor who would pledge himself to abide by the terms of her father's will. These were conditions that frightened away many an ardent wooer. For he who would win Portia's heart and hand, had to guess which of three caskets held her portrait. If he guessed aright, then Portia would be his bride; if wrong, then he was bound by oath never to reveal which casket he chose, never to marry, and to go away at once.

The caskets were of gold, silver, and lead. The gold one bore this inscription:—"Who chooseth me shall gain what many men desire"; the silver one had this:—"Who chooseth me shall get as much as he deserves"; while o n the lead one w e r e these words:—"Who chooseth me m u s t give and hazard all h e h a t h.' The Prince of Morocco, as brave as he was black, was a m o n g the first to submit to this test. He chose the gold casket, for he said neither base lead nor silver could contain her picture.

THE PRINCE OF MOROCCO.

So he chose the gold casket, and found inside the likeness of what many men desire—death.

After him came the haughty Prince of Arragon, and saying, "Let me have what I deserve—surely I

187

deserve the lady," he chose the silver one, and found inside a fool's head. "Did I deserve no more than a fool's head?" he cried.

Then at last came Bassanio, and Portia would have delayed him from making his choice from very

ANTONIO SIGNS THE BOND.

fear of his choosing wrong. For she loved him dearly, even as he loved her. "But," said Bassanio, "let me choose at once, for, as I am, I live upon the rack."

Then Portia bade her servants to bring music and play while her gallant lover made his choice. And Bassanio took the oath and walked up to the caskets—the musicians playing softly the while. "Mere outward show," he said, "is to be despised. The world is still deceived with ornament, and so no

188

gaudy gold or shining silver for me. I choose the lead casket; joy be the consequence!" And opening it, he found fair Portia's portrait inside, and he turned to her and asked if it were true that she was his.

"Yes," said Portia, "I am yours, and this house is yours, and with them I give you this ring, from which you must never part."

And Bassanio, saying that he could hardly speak for joy, found words to swear that he would never part with the ring while he lived.

Then suddenly all his happiness was dashed with sorrow, for messengers came from Venice to tell him that Antonio was ruined, and that Shylock demanded from the Duke the fulfilment of the bond, under which he was entitled to a pound of the merchant's flesh. Portia was as grieved as Bassanio to hear of the danger which threatened his friend.

"First," she said, "take me to church and make me your wife, and then go to Venice at once to help your friend. You shall take with you money enough to pay his debt twenty times over."

But when her newly-made husband had gone, Portia went after him, and arrived in Venice disguised as a lawyer, and with an introduction from a celebrated lawyer Bellario, whom the Duke of Venice had called in to decide the legal questions raised by Shylock's claim to a pound of Antonio's flesh. When the Court met, Bassanio offered Shylock twice the money borrowed, if he would withdraw his claim. But the money-lender's only answer was—

> " If every ducat in six thousand ducats
>     Were in six parts, and every part a ducat,
>     I would not draw them,— I would have my bond."

It was then that Portia arrived in her disguise, and not even her own husband knew her. The Duke gave her welcome on account of the great Bellario's introduction, and left the settlement of the case to her. Then in noble words she bade Shylock have mercy. But he was deaf to her entreaties. "I will have the pound of flesh," was his reply.

"What have you to say?" asked Portia of the merchant.

"But little," he answered; "I am armed and well prepared."

190

"The Court awards you a pound of Antonio's flesh," said Portia to the money-lender.

"Most righteous judge!" cried Shylock. "A sentence: come, prepare."

"Tarry a little. This bond gives you no right to Antonio's blood, only to his flesh. If, then, you spill a drop of his blood, all your property will be forfeited to the State. Such is the Law."

And Shylock, in his fear, said, "Then I will take Bassanio's offer."

JESSICA LEAVING HOME.

"No," said Portia sternly, "you shall have nothing but your bond. Take your pound of flesh, but remember, that if you take more or less, even by the weight of a hair, you will lose your property and your life."

Shylock now grew very much frightened. "Give me my three thousand ducats that I lent him, and let him go."

BASSANIO PARTS WITH THE RING.

Bassanio would have paid it to him, but said Portia, "No! He shall have nothing but his bond."

"You, a foreigner," she added, "have sought to take the life of a Venetian citizen, and thus by the Venetian law, your life and goods are forfeited. Down, therefore, and beg mercy of the Duke."

Thus were the tables turned, and no mercy would have been shown to Shylock, had it not been for

192

Antonio. As it was, the money-lender forfeited half his fortune to the State, and he had to settle the other half on his daughter's husband, and with this he had to be content.

Bassanio, in his gratitude to the clever lawyer, was induced to part with the ring his wife had given him, and with which he had promised never to part, and when on his return to Belmont he confessed as much to Portia, she seemed very angry, and vowed she would not be friends with him until she had her ring again. But at last she told him that it was she who, in the disguise of the lawyer, had saved his friend's life, and got the ring from him. So Bassanio was forgiven, and made happier than ever, to know how rich a prize he had drawn in the lottery of the caskets.

POET READING TO TIMON.

## TIMON OF ATHENS

FOUR hundred years before the birth of Christ, a man lived in Athens whose generosity was not only great, but absurd. He was very rich, but no worldly wealth was enough for a man who spent and gave like Timon. If anybody gave Timon a horse, he received from Timon twenty better horses. If anybody borrowed money of Timon and offered to repay it, Timon was offended. If a poet had written a poem and Timon had time to read it, he would be sure to buy it; and a painter had only to

194

hold up his canvas in front of Timon to receive double its market price.

Flavius, his steward, looked with dismay at his reckless mode of life. When Timon's house was full of noisy lords drinking and spilling costly wine, Flavius would sit in a cellar and cry. He would say to himself, "There are ten thousand candles burning in this house, and each of those singers braying in the concert-room costs a poor man's yearly income a night"; and he would remember a terrible thing said by Apemantus, one of his master's friends, "O what a number of men eat Timon, and Timon sees them not!"

Of course, Timon was much praised.

A jeweler who sold him a diamond pretended that it was not quite perfect till Timon wore it. "You mend the jewel by wearing it," he said. Timon gave the diamond to a lord called Sempronius, and the lord exclaimed, "O, he's the very soul of bounty." "Timon is infinitely dear to me," said another lord, called Lucullus, to whom he gave a beautiful horse; and other Athenians paid him compliments as sweet.

But when Apemantus had listened to some of

them, he said, "I'm going to knock out an honest Athenian's brains."

"You will die for that," said Timon.

"Then I shall die for doing nothing," said Apemantus. And now you know what a joke was like four hundred years before Christ.

This Apemantus was a frank despiser of mankind, but a healthy one, because he was not unhappy. In this mixed world anyone with a number of acquaintances knows a person who talks bitterly of men, but does not shun them, and boasts that he is never deceived by their fine speeches, and is inwardly cheerful and proud. Apemantus was a man like that.

Timon, you will be surprised to hear, became much worse than Apemantus, after the dawning of a day which we call Quarter Day.

Quarter Day is the day when bills pour in. The grocer, the butcher, and the baker are all thinking of their debtors on that day, and the wise man has saved enough money to be ready for them. But Timon had not; and he did not only owe money for food. He owed it for jewels and horses and fur-

niture; and, worst of all, he owed it to money-lend-
ers, who expected him to pay twice as much as he
had borrowed.

Quarter Day is a day when promises to pay are
scorned, and on that day Timon was asked for a
large sum of money. "Sell some land," he said to
his steward.
"You have no
land," was the
reply. "Non-
sense! I had
a hundred
thousand
acres," said
Timon. "You
could have

PAINTER SHOWING TIMON A PICTURE.

spent the price of the world if you had possessed it,"
said Flavius.

"Borrow some then," said Timon; "try Ventidius." He thought of Ventidius because he had
once got Ventidius out of prison by paying a
creditor of this young man. Ventidius was now
rich. Timon trusted in his gratitude. But not

for all; so much did he owe! Servants were despatched with requests for loans of money to several friends:

One servant (Flaminius) went to Lucullus. When he was announced Lucullus said, "A gift, I warrant. I dreamt of a silver jug and basin last night." Then, changing his tone, "How is that honorable, free-hearted, perfect gentleman, your master, eh?"

"Well in health, sir," replied Flaminius.

"And what have you got there under your cloak?" asked Lucullus, jovially.

"Faith, sir, nothing but an empty box, which, on my master's behalf, I beg you to fill with money, sir."

"La! la! la!" said Lucullus, who could not pretend to mean, "Ha! ha! ha!" "Your master's one fault is that he is too fond of giving parties. I've warned him that it was expensive. Now, look here, Flaminius, you know this is no time to lend money without security, so suppose you act like a good boy and tell him that I was not at home. Here's three solidares for yourself."

"Back, wretched money," cried Flaminius, "to him who worships you!"

Others of Timon's friends were tried and found stingy. Amongst them was Sempronius.

"Hum," he said to Timon's servant, "has he asked Ventidius? Ventidius is beholden to him."

"He refused."

"Well, have you asked Lucullus?"

"He refused."

"A poor compliment to apply to me last of all," said Sempronius, in affected anger. "If he had sent to me at first, I would gladly have lent him money, but I'm not going to be such a fool as to lend him any now."

"Your lordship makes a good villain," said the servant.

When Timon found that his friends were so mean, he took advantage of a lull in his storm of creditors to invite Ventidius and Company to a banquet. Flavius was horrified, but Ventidius and Company were not in the least ashamed, and they assembled accordingly in Timon's house, and said to one another that their princely host had been jesting with them.

199

"I had to put off an important engagement in order to come here," said Lucullus; "but who could refuse Timon?"

"It was a real grief to me to be without ready money when he asked for some," said Sempronius.

"The same here," chimed in a third lord.

Timon now appeared, and his guests vied with one another in apologies and compliments. Inwardly sneering, Timon was gracious to them all.

"NOTHING BUT AN EMPTY BOX."

In the banqueting hall was a table resplendent with covered dishes. Mouths watered. These summer-friends loved good food.

"Be seated, worthy friends," said Timon. He

200

then prayed aloud to the gods of Greece. "Give each man enough," he said, "for if you, who are our gods, were to borrow of men they would cease to adore you. Let men love the joint more than the host. Let every score of guests contain twenty villains. Bless my friends as much as they have blessed me. Uncover the dishes, dogs, and lap!"

The hungry lords were too much surprised by this speech to resent it. They thought Timon was unwell, and, although he had called them dogs, they uncovered the dishes.

There was nothing in them but warm water.

"May you never see a better feast," wished Timon. "I wash off the flatteries with which you plastered me and sprinkle you with your villainy." With these words he threw the water into his guests' faces, and then he pelted them with the dishes. Having thus ended the banquet, he went into an outhouse, seized a spade, and quitted Athens for ever.

His next dwelling was a cave near the sea.

Of all his friends, the only one who had not refused him aid was a handsome soldier named Alcibiades, and he had not been asked because, having quarreled with the Government of Athens, he had left that town. The thought that Alcibiades might have proved a true friend did not soften Timon's bitter feeling. He was too weak-minded to discern the fact that good cannot be far from evil in this mixed world. He determined to see nothing better in all mankind than the ingratitude of Ventidius and the meanness of Lucullus.

He became a vegetarian, and talked pages to himself as he dug in the earth for food.

One day, when he was digging for roots near the shore, his spade struck gold. If he had been a wise man he would have enriched himself quickly, and returned to Athens to live in comfort. But the sight of the gold vein gave no joy but only scorn to Timon. "This yellow slave," he said, "will make and break religions. It will make black white and foul fair. It will buy murder and bless the accursed."

He was still ranting when Alcibiades, now an enemy of Athens, approached with his soldiers and two beautiful women who cared for nothing but pleasure.

202

Timon was so changed by his bad thoughts and rough life that Alcibiades did not recognize him at first.

"Who are you?" he asked.

"A beast, as you are," was the reply.

Alcibiades knew his voice, and offered him help and money. But Timon would none of it, and began to insult the women. They, however, when they found he had discovered a gold mine, cared not a jot for his opinion of them, but said, "Give us some gold, good Timon. Have you more?"

With further insults, Timon filled their aprons with gold ore.

"Farewell," said Alcibiades, who deemed that Timon's wits were lost; and then his disciplined soldiers left without profit the mine which could have paid their wages, and marched towards Athens.

Timon continued to dig and curse, and affected great delight when he dug up a root and discovered that it was not a grape.

Just then Apemantus appeared. "I am told that you imitate me," said Apemantus.

"Only," said Timon, "because you haven't a dog which I can imitate."

"You are revenging yourself on your friends by punishing yourself," said Apemantus. "That is very silly, for they live just as comfortably as they

TIMON GROWS SULLEN.

ever did. I am sorry that a fool should imitate me."

"If I were like you," said Timon, "I should throw myself away."

"You have done so," sneered Apemantus. "Will the cold brook make you a good morning drink, or an east wind warm your clothes as a valet would?"

"Off with you!" said Timon; but Apemantus stayed a while longer and told him he had a passion for extremes, which was true. Apemantus even made a pun, but there was no good laughter to be got out of Timon.

Finally, they lost their temper like two schoolboys, and Timon said he was sorry to lose the stone which he flung at Apemantus, who left him with an evil wish.

This was almost an "at home" day for Timon, for when Apemantus had departed, he was visited by some robbers. They wanted gold.

"You want too much," said Timon. "Here are water, roots and berries."

"We are not birds and pigs," said a robber.

"No, you are cannibals," said Timon. "Take the gold, then, and may it poison you! Henceforth rob one another."

He spoke so frightfully to them that, though they went away with full pockets, they almost repented of their trade.

205

His last visitor on that day of visits was his good steward Flavius. "My dearest master!" cried he.

"Away! What are you?" said Timon.

"Have you forgotten me, sir?" asked Flavius, mournfully.

"I have forgotten all men," was the reply; "and if you'll allow that you are a man, I have forgotten you."

"I was your honest servant," said Flavius.

"Nonsense! I never had an honest man about me," retorted Timon.

Flavius began to cry.

"What! shedding tears?" said Timon. "Come nearer, then. I will love you because you are a woman, and unlike men, who only weep when they laugh or beg."

They talked awhile; then Timon said, "Yon gold is mine. I will make you rich, Flavius, if you promise me to live by yourself and hate mankind. I will make you very rich if you promise me that you will see the flesh slide off the beggar's bones before you feed him, and let the debtor die in jail before you pay his debt."

Flavius simply said, "Let me stay to comfort you, my master."

"If you dislike cursing, leave me," replied Timon, and he turned his back on Flavius, who went sadly back to Athens, too much accustomed to obedience to force his services upon his ailing master.

The steward had accepted nothing, but a report got about that a mighty nugget of gold had been given him by his former master, and Timon therefore received more visitors. They were a painter and a poet, whom he had patronized in his prosperity.

"Hail, worthy Timon!" said the poet. "We heard with astonishment how your friends deserted you. No whip's large enough for their backs!"

"We have come," put in the painter, "to offer our services."

"You've heard that I have gold," said Timon.

"There was a report," said the painter, blushing; "but my friend and I did not come for that."

"Good honest men!" jeered Timon. "All the same, you shall have plenty of gold if you will rid me of two villains."

"Name them," said his two visitors in one breath.

"Both of you!" answered Timon. Giving the painter a whack with a big stick, he said, "Put that into your palette and make money out of it." Then he gave a whack to the poet, and said, "Make a poem out of that and get paid for it. There's gold for you."

They hurriedly withdrew.

Finally Timon was visited by two senators who, now that Athens was threatened by Alcibiades, desired to have on their side this bitter noble whose gold might help the foe.

"Forget your injuries," said the first senator. "Athens offers you dignities whereby you may honorably live."

"Athens confesses that your merit was overlooked, and wishes to atone, and more than atone, for her forgetfulness," said the second senator.

"Worthy senators," replied Timon, in his grim way, "I am almost weeping; you touch me so! All I need are the eyes of a woman and the heart of a fool."

But the senators were patriots. They believed

that this bitter man could save Athens, and they would not quarrel with him. "Be our captain," they said, "and lead Athens against Alcibiades, who threatens to destroy her."

"Let him destroy the Athenians too, for all I care," said Timon; and seeing an evil despair in his face, they left him.

The senators returned to Athens, and soon afterwards trumpets were blown before its walls. Upon the walls they stood and listened to Alcibiades, who told them that wrong-doers should quake in their easy chairs. They looked at his confident army, and were convinced that Athens must yield if he assaulted it, therefore they used the voice that strikes deeper than arrows.

"These walls of ours were built by the hands of men who never wronged you, Alcibiades," said the first senator.

"Enter," said the second senator, "and slay every tenth man, if your revenge needs human flesh."

"Spare the cradle," said the first senator.

"I ask only justice," said Alcibiades. "If you

admit my army, I will inflict the penalty of your own laws upon any soldier who breaks them."

At that moment a soldier approached Alcibiades, and said, "My noble general, Timon is dead." He handed Alcibiades a sheet of wax, saying, "He is buried by the sea, on the beach, and over his grave is a stone with letters on it which I cannot read, and therefore I have impressed them on wax."

Alcibiades read from the sheet of wax this couplet—

"Here lie I, Timon, who, alive, all living men did hate.
    Pass by and say your worst; but pass, and stay not here your gait."

"Dead, then, is noble Timon," said Alcibiades; and he entered Athens with an olive branch instead of a sword.

So it was one of Timon's friends who was generous in a greater matter than Timon's need; yet are the sorrow and rage of Timon remembered as a warning lest another ingratitude should arise to turn love into hate.

OTHELLO TELLING DESDEMONA HIS ADVENTURES.

## OTHELLO

FOUR hundred years ago there lived in Venice an ensign named Iago, who hated his general, Othello, for not making him a lieutenant. Instead of Iago, who was strongly recommended, Othello had chosen Michael Cassio, whose smooth tongue had helped him to win the heart of Desdemona. Iago had a friend called Roderigo, who supplied him with money and felt he could not be happy unless Desdemona was his wife.

Othello was a Moor, but of so dark a complexion that his enemies called him a Blackamoor. His life had been hard and exciting. He had been vanquished in battle and sold into slavery; and he had been a great traveler and seen men whose shoulders were higher than their heads. Brave as a lion, he had one great fault—jealousy. His love was a terrible selfishness. To love a woman meant with him to possess her as absolutely as he possessed something that did not live and think. The story of Othello is a story of jealousy.

One night Iago told Roderigo that Othello had carried off Desdemona without the knowledge of her father, Brabantio. He persuaded Roderigo to arouse Brabantio, and when that senator appeared Iago told him of Desdemona's elopement in the most unpleasant way. Though he was Othello's officer, he termed him a thief and a Barbary horse.

Brabantio accused Othello before the Duke of Venice of using sorcery to fascinate his daughter, but Othello said that the only sorcery he used was his voice, which told Desdemona his adventures and hair-breadth escapes. Desdemona was led into the council-chamber, and she explained how she could love Othello despite his almost black face by saying, "I saw Othello's visage in his mind."

As Othello had married Desdemona, and she was glad to be his wife, there was no more to be said against him, especially as the Duke wished him to go to Cyprus to defend it against the Turks. Othello was quite ready to go, and Desdemona, who pleaded to go with him, was permitted to join him at Cyprus.

Othello's feelings on landing in this island were intensely joyful. "Oh, my

OTHELLO.

213

sweet," he said to Desdemona, who arrived with Iago, his wife, and Roderigo before him, "I hardly know what I say to you. I am in love with my own happiness."

News coming presently that the Turkish fleet was out of action, he proclaimed a festival in Cyprus from five to eleven at night.

Cassio was on duty in the Castle where Othello ruled Cyprus, so Iago decided to make the lieutenant drink too much. He had some difficulty, as Cassio knew that wine soon went to his head, but servants brought wine into the room where Cassio was, and Iago sang a drinking song, and so Cassio lifted a glass too often to the health of the general.

When Cassio was inclined to be quarrelsome, Iago told Roderigo to say something unpleasant to him. Cassio cudgeled Roderigo, who ran into the presence of Montano, the ex-governor. Montano civilly interceded for Roderigo, but received so rude an answer from Cassio that he said, "Come, come, you're drunk!" Cassio then wounded him, and Iago sent Roderigo out to scare the town with a cry of mutiny.

The uproar aroused Othello, who, on learning its cause, said, "Cassio, I love thee, but never more be officer of mine."

On Cassio and Iago being alone together, the disgraced man moaned about his reputation. Iago said reputation and humbug were the same thing. "O God," exclaimed Cassio, without heeding him, "that men should put an enemy in their mouths to steal away their brains!"

Iago advised him to beg Desdemona to ask Othello to pardon him. Cassio was pleased with the advice, and next morning made his request to Desdemona in the garden of the castle. She was kindness itself, and said, "Be merry, Cassio, for I would rather die than forsake your cause."

Cassio at that moment saw Othello advancing with Iago, and retired hurriedly.

Iago said, "I don't like that."

"What did you say?" asked Othello, who felt that he had meant something unpleasant, but Iago pretended he had said nothing. "Was not that Cassio who went from my wife?" asked Othello, and Iago, who knew that it was Cassio and why it was Cassio,

215

said, "I cannot think it was Cassio who stole away in that guilty manner."

Desdemona told Othello that it was grief and humility which made Cassio retreat at his approach. She reminded him how Cassio had taken his part when she was still heart-free, and found fault with her Moorish lover. Othello was melted, and said, "I will deny thee nothing," but Desdemona told him that what she asked was as much for his good as dining.

Desdemona left the garden, and Iago asked if it was really true that Cassio had known Desdemona before her marriage.

"Yes," said Othello.

"Indeed," said Iago, as though something that had mystified him was now very clear.

"Is he not honest?" demanded Othello, and Iago repeated the adjective inquiringly, as though he were afraid to say "No."

"What do you mean?" insisted Othello.

To this Iago would only say the flat opposite of what he said to Cassio. He had told Cassio that reputation was humbug. To Othello he said, "Who steals my purse steals trash, but he who filches from me my good name ruins me."

At this Othello almost leapt into the air, and Iago was so confident of his jealousy that he ventured to warn him against it. Yes, it was no other than Iago who called jealousy "the green-eyed monster which doth mock the meat it feeds on."

Iago having given jealousy one blow, proceeded to feed it with the remark that Desdemona deceived her father when she eloped with Othello. "If she deceived him, why not you?" was his meaning.

Presently Desdemona re-entered to tell Othello that dinner was ready. She saw that he was ill at ease. He explained it by a pain in his forehead. Desdemona then produced a handkerchief, which Othello had given her. A prophetess, two hundred years old, had made this handkerchief from the silk of sacred silkworms, dyed it in a liquid prepared from the hearts of maidens, and embroidered it with strawberries. Gentle Desdemona thought of it simply as a cool, soft thing for a throbbing brow; she knew of no spell upon it that would work destruction for her who lost it. "Let me tie it round

217

your head," she said to Othello; "you will be well in an hour." But Othello pettishly said it was too small, and let it fall. Desdemona and he then went indoors to dinner, and Emilia picked up the hand-kerchief which Iago had often asked her to steal.

She was look-ing at it when Iago came in. After a few words about it he snatched it from her, and bade her leave him.

In the garden he was joined

THE DRINK OF WINE.

by Othello, who seemed hungry for the worst lies he could offer. He therefore told Othello that he had seen Cassio wipe his mouth with a handkerchief, which, because it was spotted with strawberries, he

218

guessed to be one that Othello had given his wife.

The unhappy Moor went mad with fury, and Iago bade the heavens witness that he devoted his hand and heart and brain to Othello's service. "I accept your love," said Othello. "Within three days let me hear that Cassio is dead."

Iago's next step was to leave Desdemona's handkerchief in Cassio's room. Cassio saw it, and knew it was not his, but he liked the strawberry pattern on it, and he gave it to his sweetheart Bianca and asked her to copy it for him.

Iago's next move was to induce Othello, who had been bullying Desdemona about the handkerchief, to play the eavesdropper to a conversation between Cassio and himself. His intention was to talk about Cassio's sweetheart, and allow Othello to suppose that the lady spoken of was Desdemona.

"How are you, lieutenant?" asked Iago when Cassio appeared.

"The worse for being called what I am not," replied Cassio, gloomily.

"Keep on reminding Desdemona, and you'll soon be restored," said Iago, adding, in a tone too low

219

for Othello to hear, "If Bianca could set the matter right, how quickly it would mend!"

"Alas! poor rogue," said Cassio, "I really think she loves me," and like the talkative coxcomb he was, Cassio was led on to boast of Bianca's fondness for him, while Othello imagined, with choked rage, that he prattled of Desdemona, and thought, "I see your nose, Cassio, but not the dog I shall throw it to."

Othello was still spying when Bianca entered, boiling over with the idea that Cassio, whom she considered her property, had asked her to copy the embroidery on the handkerchief of a new sweetheart. She tossed him the handkerchief with scornful words, and Cassio departed with her.

Othello had seen Bianca, who was in station lower, in beauty and speech inferior far, to Desdemona, and he began in spite of himself to praise his wife to the villain before him. He praised her skill with the needle, her voice that could "sing the savageness out of a bear," her wit, her sweetness, the fairness of her skin. Every time he praised her Iago said something that made him remember his anger and utter it foully, and yet he must needs praise her, and say, "The pity of it, Iago! O Iago, the pity of it, Iago!"

There was never in all Iago's villainy one moment of wavering. If there had been he might have wavered then.

"Strangle her," he said; and "Good, good!" said his miserable dupe.

The pair were still talking murder when Desdemona appeared with a relative of Desdemona's father, called Lodovico, who bore a letter for Othello from the Duke of Venice. The letter recalled Othello from Cyprus, and gave the governorship to Cassio.

Luckless Desdemona seized this unhappy moment to urge once more the suit of Cassio.

"Fire and brimstone!" shouted Othello.

"It may be the letter agitates him," explained Lodovico to Desdemona, and he told her what it contained.

"I am glad," said Desdemona. It was the first bitter speech that Othello's unkindness had wrung out of her.

"I am glad to see you lose your temper," said Othello.

221

"Why, sweet Othello?" she asked, sarcastically; and Othello slapped her face.

Now was the time for Desdemona to have saved her life by separation, but she knew not her peril—

CASSIO GIVES BIANCA THE HANDKERCHIEF.

only that her love was wounded to the core. "I have not deserved this," she said, and the tears rolled slowly down her face.

Lodovico was shocked and disgusted. "My lord," he said, "this would not be believed in Venice. Make her amends;" but, like a madman talking in his nightmare, Othello poured out his foul thought in ugly speech, and roared, "Out of my sight!"

"I will not stay to offend you," said his wife, but she lingered even in going, and only when he shouted "Avaunt!" did she leave her husband and his guests.

Othello then invited Lodovico to supper, adding, "You are welcome, sir, to Cyprus. Goats and monkeys!" Without waiting for a reply he left the company.

Distinguished visitors detest being obliged to look on at family quarrels, and dislike being called either goats or monkeys, and Lodovico asked Iago for an explanation.

True to himself, Iago, in a round-about way, said that Othello was worse than he seemed, and advised them to study his behavior and save him from the discomfort of answering any more questions.

He proceeded to tell Roderigo to murder Cassio. Roderigo was out of tune with his friend. He had given Iago quantities of jewels for Desdemona without effect; Desdemona had seen none of them, for Iago was a thief.

Iago smoothed him with a lie, and when Cassio was leaving Bianca's house, Roderigo wounded him, and was wounded in return. Cassio shouted, and Lodovico and a friend came running up. Cassio pointed out Roderigo as his assailant, and Iago, hoping to rid himself of an inconvenient friend, called him "Villain!" and stabbed him, but not to death.

At the Castle, Desdemona was in a sad mood. She told Emilia that she must leave her; her husband wished it. "Dismiss me!" exclaimed Emilia. "It was his bidding," said Desdemona; "we must not displease him now."

She sang a song which a girl had sung whose lover had been base to her—a song of a maiden crying by that tree whose boughs droop as though it weeps, and she went to bed and slept.

She woke with her husband's wild eyes upon her. "Have you prayed to-night?" he asked; and he told this blameless and sweet woman to ask God's par-

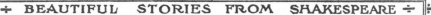

don for any sin she might have on her conscience. "I would not kill thy soul," he said.

He told her that Cassio had confessed, but she

DESDEMONA WEEPING.

knew Cassio had nought to confess that concerned her. She said that Cassio could not say anything that would damage her. Othello said his mouth was stopped.

225

Then Desdemona wept, but with violent words, in spite of all her pleading, Othello pressed upon her throat and mortally hurt her.

Then with boding heart came Emilia, and besought entrance at the door, and Othello unlocked it, and a voice came from the bed saying, "A guiltless death I die."

"Who did it?" cried Emilia; and the voice said, "Nobody—I myself. Farewell!"

"'Twas I that killed her," said Othello.

He poured out his evidence by that sad bed to the people who came running in, Iago among them; but when he spoke of the handkerchief, Emilia told the truth.

And Othello knew. "Are there no stones in heaven but thunderbolts?" he exclaimed, and ran at Iago, who gave Emilia her death-blow and fled.

But they brought him back, and the death that came to him later on was a relief from torture.

They would have taken Othello back to Venice to try him there, but he escaped them on his sword. "A word or two before you go," he said to the Venetians in the chamber. "Speak of me as I was—

no better, no worse. Say I cast away the pearl of pearls, and wept with these hard eyes; and say that, when in Aleppo years ago I saw a Turk beating a Venetian, I took him by the throat and smote him thus."

With his own hand he stabbed himself to the heart; and ere he died his lips touched the face of Desdemona with despairing love.

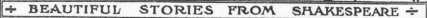

## THE TAMING OF THE SHREW

THERE lived in Padua a gentleman named Baptista, who had two fair daughters. The eldest, Katharine, was so very cross and ill-tempered, and unmannerly, that no one ever dreamed of marrying her, while her siter, Bianca, was so sweet and pretty, and pleasant-spoken, that more than one suitor asked her father for her hand. But Baptista said the elder daughter must marry first.

So Bianca's suitors decided among themselves to try and get some one to marry Katharine—and then the father could at least be got to listen to their suit for Bianca.

A gentleman from Verona, named Petruchio, was the one they thought of, and, half in jest, they asked him if he would marry Katharine, the disagreeable scold. Much to their surprise he said yes, that was just the sort of wife for him, and if Katharine were handsome and rich, he himself would undertake soon to make her good-tempered.

Petruchio began by asking Baptista's permission to pay court to his gentle daughter Katharine— and Baptista was obliged to own that she was anything but gentle. And just then her music master rushed in, complaining that the naughty girl had broken her lute over his head, because he told her she was not playing correctly.

THE MUSIC MASTER.

"Never mind," said Petruchio, "I love her better than ever, and long to have some chat with her."

229

When Katharine came, he said, "Good-morrow, Kate—for that, I hear, is your name."

"You've only heard half," said Katharine, rudely.

"Oh, no," said Petruchio, "they call you plain Kate, and bonny Kate, and sometimes Kate the shrew, and so, hearing your mildness praised in every town, and your beauty too, I ask you for my wife."

"Your wife!" cried Kate. "Never!" She said some extremely disagreeable things to him, and, I am sorry to say, ended by boxing his ears.

"If you do that again, I'll cuff you," he said quietly; and still protested, with many compliments, that he would marry none but her.

When Baptista came back, he asked at once—

"How speed you with my daughter?"

"How should I speed but well," replied Petruchio—"how, but well?"

"How now, daughter Katharine?" the father went on.

"I don't think," said Katharine, angrily, "you are acting a father's part in wishing me to marry this mad-cap ruffian."

"Ah!" said Petruchio, "you and all the world would talk amiss of her. You should see how kind she is to me when we are alone. In short, I will go off to Venice to buy fine things for our wedding— for—kiss me, Kate! we will be married on Sunday."

With that, Katharine flounced out of the room by one door in a violent temper, and he, laughing, went out by the other. But whether she fell in love with Petruchio, or whether she was only glad to meet a man who was not afraid of her, or whether she was flattered that, in spite of her rough words and spiteful usage, he still desired her for his wife— she did indeed marry him on Sunday, as he had sworn she should.

To vex and humble Katharine's naughty, proud spirit, he was late at the wedding, and when he came, came wearing such shabby clothes that she was ashamed to be seen with him. His servant was dressed in the same shabby way, and the horses they rode were the sport of everyone they passed.

And, after the marriage, when should have been the wedding breakfast, Petruchio carried his wife away, not allowing her to eat or drink—saying that

231

she was his now, and he could do as he liked with her.

And his manner was so violent, and he behaved all through his wedding in so mad and dreadful a manner, that Katharine trembled and went with

KATHARINE BOXES THE SERVANT'S EARS.

him. He mounted her on a stumbling, lean, old horse, and they journeyed by rough muddy ways to Petruchio's house, he scolding and snarling all the way.

She was terribly tired when she reached her new home, but Petruchio was determined that she should neither eat nor sleep that night, for he had made up his mind to teach his bad-tempered wife a lesson she would never forget.

So he welcomed her kindly to his house, but when supper was served he found fault with everything —the meat was burnt, he said, and ill-served, and he loved her far too much to let her eat anything but the best. At last Katharine, tired out with her journey, went supperless to bed. Then her husband, still telling her how he loved her, and how anxious he was that she should sleep well, pulled her bed to pieces, throwing the pillows and bed-clothes on the floor, so that she could not go to bed at all, and still kept growling and scolding at the servants so that Kate might see how unbeautiful a thing ill-temper was.

The next day, too, Katharine's food was all found fault with, and caught away before she could touch a mouthful, and she was sick and giddy for want of sleep. Then she said to one of the servants—

"I pray thee go and get me some repast. I care not what."

233

"What say you to a neat's foot?" said the servant.

Katharine said "Yes," eagerly; but the servant, who was in his master's secret, said he feared it was not good for hasty-tempered people. Would she like tripe?

"Bring it me," said Katharine.

"I don't think *that* is good for hasty-tempered people," said the servant. "What do you say to a dish of beef and mustard?"

"I love it," said Kate.

"But mustard is too hot."

"Why, then, the beef, and let the mustard go," cried Katharine, who was getting hungrier and hungrier.

"No," said the servant, "you must have the mustard, or you get no beef from me."

"Then," cried Katharine, losing patience, "let it be both, or one, or anything thou wilt."

"Why, then," said the servant, "the mustard without the beef!"

Then Katharine saw he was making fun of her, and boxed *his* ears.

Just then Petruchio brought her some food—but she had scarcely begun to satisfy her hunger, before he called for the tailor to bring her new clothes, and the table was cleared, leaving her still hungry. Katharine was pleased with the pretty new dress and cap that the tailor had made for her, but Petru-

PETRUCHIO FINDS FAULT WITH THE SUPPER.

chio found fault with everything, flung the cap and gown on the floor vowing his dear wife should not wear any such foolish things.

"I will have them," cried Katharine. "All gentlewomen wear such caps as these—"

"When you are gentle you shall have one too," he answered, "and not till then." When he had

235

driven away the tailor with angry words—but privately asking his friend to see him paid—Petruchio said—

"Come, Kate, let's go to your father's, shabby as we are, for as the sun breaks through the darkest clouds, so honor peereth in the meanest habit.  It is about seven o'clock now.  We shall easily get there by dinner-time."

"It's nearly two," said Kate, but civilly enough, for she had grown to see that she could not bully her husband, as she had done her father and her sister; "it's nearly two, and it will be supper-time before we get there."

"It shall be seven," said Petruchio, obstinately, "before I start.  Why, whatever I say or do, or think, you do nothing but contradict.  I won't go to-day, and before I do go, it shall be what o'clock I say it is."

At last they started for her father's house. "Look at the moon," said he.

"It's the sun," said Katharine, and indeed it was.

"I say it is the moon.  Contradicting again!  It

236

shall be sun or moon, or whatever I choose, or I won't take you to your father's."

Then Katharine gave in, once and for all. "What you will have it named," she said, "it is, and so it shall be so for Katharine." And so it was, for from that moment Katharine felt that she had met her master, and never again showed her naughty tempers to him, or anyone else.

So they journeyed on to Baptista's house, and arriving there, they found all folks keeping Bianca's wedding feast, and that of another newly married couple, Hortensio and his wife. They were made welcome, and sat down to the feast, and all was merry, save that Hortensio's wife, seeing Katharine subdued to her husband, thought she could safely say many disagreeable things, that in the old days, when Katharine was free and froward, she would not have dared to say. But Katharine answered with such spirit and such moderation, that she turned the laugh against the new bride.

After dinner, when the ladies had retired, Baptista joined in a laugh against Petruchio, saying-

237

"Now in good sadness, son Petruchio, I fear you have got the veriest shrew of all."

"You are wrong," said Petruchio, "let me prove it to you. Each of us shall send a message to his wife, desiring her to come to him, and the one whose wife comes most readily shall win a wager which we will agree on."

The others said yes readily enough, for each thought his own wife the most dutiful, and each thought he was quite sure to win the wager.

They proposed a wager of twenty crowns.

"Twenty crowns," said Petruchio, "I'll venture so much on my hawk or hound, but twenty times as much upon my wife."

"A hundred then," cried Lucentio, Bianca's husband.

"Content," cried the others.

Then Lucentio sent a message to the fair Bianca bidding her to come to him. And Baptista said he was certain his daughter would come. But the servant coming back, said—

"Sir, my mistress is busy, and she cannot come."

"There's an answer for you," said Petruchio.

"You may think yourself fortunate if your wife does not send you a worse."

"I hope, better," Petruchio answered. Then Hortensio said—

"Go and entreat my wife to come to me at once."

"Oh—if you *entreat* her," said Petruchio.

"I am afraid," answered Hortensio, sharply, "do what you can, yours will not be entreated."

But now the servant came in, and said—

"She says you are playing some jest, she will not come."

"Better and better," cried Petruchio; "now go to your mistress and say I *command* her to come to me."

They all began to laugh, saying they knew what her answer would be, and that she would not come.

Then suddenly Baptista cried—

"Here comes Katharine!" And sure enough—there she was.

"What do you wish, sir?" she asked her husband.

"Where are your sister and Hortensio's wife?"

"Talking by the parlor fire."

"Fetch them here."

239

When she was gone to fetch them, Lucentio said—

"Here is a wonder!"

"I wonder what it means," said Hortensio.

"It means peace," said Petruchio, "and love, and quiet life."

"Well," said Baptista, "you have won the wager, and I will add another twenty thousand crowns to her dowry—another dowry for another daughter— for she is as changed as if she were someone else."

So Petruchio won his wager, and had in Katharine always a loving wife and true, and now he had broken her proud and angry spirit he loved her well, and there was nothing ever but love between those two. And so they lived happy ever afterwards.

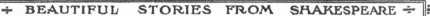

## MEASURE FOR MEASURE

**M**ORE centuries ago than I care to say, the people of Vienna were governed too mildly. The reason was that the reigning Duke Vicentio was excessively good-natured, and disliked to see offenders made unhappy.

The consequence was that the number of ill-behaved persons in Vienna was enough to make the Duke shake his head in sorrow when his chief secretary showed him it at the end of a list. He decided, therefore, that wrongdoers must be punished. But popularity was dear to him. He knew that, if he were suddenly strict after being lax, he would cause people to call him a tyrant. For this reason he told his Privy Council that he must go to Poland on important business of state. "I have chosen Angelo to rule in my absence," said he.

Now this Angelo, although he appeared to be noble, was really a mean man. He had promised

241

to marry a girl called Mariana, and now would have nothing to say to her, because her dowry had been lost. So poor Mariana lived forlornly, waiting every day for the footstep of her stingy lover, and loving him still.

Having appointed Angelo his deputy, the Duke went to a friar called Thomas and asked him for a friar's dress and instruction in the art of giving religious counsel, for he did not intend to go to Poland, but to stay at home and see how Angelo governed.

Angelo had not been a day in office when he condemned to death a young man named Claudio for an act of rash selfishness which nowadays would only be punished by severe reproof.

Claudio had a queer friend called Lucio, and Lucio saw a chance of freedom for Claudio if Claudio's beautiful sister Isabella would plead with Angelo.

Isabella was at that time living in a nunnery. Nobody had won her heart, and she thought she would like to become a sister, or nun.

Meanwhile Claudio did not lack an advocate.

An ancient lord, Escalus, was for leniency. "Let us cut a little, but not kill," he said. "This gentleman had a most noble father."

Angelo was unmoved. "If twelve men find me guilty, I ask no more mercy than is in the law."

Angelo then ordered the Provost to see that Claudio was executed at nine the next morning.

After the issue of this order Angelo was told that the sister of the condemned man desired to see him.

"Admit her," said Angelo.

On entering with Lucio, the beautiful girl said, "I am a woeful suitor to your Honor."

"Well?" said Angelo.

She colored at his chill monosyllable and the ascending red increased the beauty of her face. "I have a brother who is condemned to die," she continued. "Condemn the fault, I pray you, and spare my brother."

"Every fault," said Angelo, "is condemned before it is committed. A fault cannot suffer. Justice would be void if the committer of a fault went free."

243

She would have left the court if Lucio had not whispered to her, "You are too cold; you could not speak more tamely if you wanted a pin."

So Isabella attacked Angelo again, and when he  said, "I will not pardon him," she was not discouraged, and when he said, "He's sentenced; 'tis too late," she returned to the assult. But all her fighting was with reasons, and with reasons she could not prevail over the Deputy.

THE DUKE IN THE FRIAR'S DRESS.

She told him that nothing becomes power like mercy. She told him that humanity receives and requires mercy from Heaven, that it was good to have gigantic strength, and bad to use it like a giant. She told him that lightning rives the oak

244

and spares the myrtle. She bade him look for fault in his own breast, and if he found one, to refrain from making it an argument against her brother's life.

Angelo found a fault in his breast at that moment. He loved Isabella's beauty, and was tempted to do for her beauty what he would not do for the love of man.

He appeared to relent, for he said, "Come to me to-morrow before noon."

She had, at any rate, succeeded in prolonging her brother's life for a few hours.

In her absence Angelo's conscience rebuked him for trifling with his judicial duty.

When Isabella called on him the second time, he said, "Your brother cannot live."

Isabella was painfully astonished, but all she said was, "Even so. Heaven keep your Honor."

But as she turned to go, Angelo felt that his duty and honor were slight in comparison with the loss of her.

"Give me your love," he said, "and Claudio shall be freed."

"Before I would marry you, he should die if he had twenty heads to lay upon the block," said Isabella, for she saw then that he was not the just man he pretended to be.

So she went to her brother in prison, to inform him that he must die. At first he was boastful, and promised to hug the darkness of death. But when he clearly understood that his sister could buy his life by marrying Angelo, he felt his life more valuable than her happiness, and he exclaimed, "Sweet sister, let me live."

"O faithless coward! O dishonest wretch!" she cried.

At this moment the Duke came forward, in the habit of a friar, to request some speech with Isabella. He called himself Friar Lodowick.

The Duke then told her that Angelo was affianced to Mariana, whose love-story he related. He then asked her to consider this plan. Let Mariana, in the dress of Isabella, go closely veiled to Angelo, and say, in a voice resembling Isabella's, that if Claudio were spared she would marry him. Let her take the ring from Angelo's little finger, that it might be afterwards proved that his visitor was Mariana.

Isabella had, of course, a great respect for friars, who are as nearly like nuns as men can be. She agreed, therefore, to the Duke's plan. They were to meet again at the moated grange, Mariana's house.

ISABELLA PLEADS WITH ANGELO.

In the street the Duke saw Lucio, who, seeing a man dressed like a friar, called out, "What news of the Duke, friar?" "I have none," said the Duke.

Lucio then told the Duke some stories about Angelo. Then he told one about the Duke. The

Duke contradicted him. Lucio was provoked, and called the Duke "a shallow, ignorant fool," though he pretended to love him. "The Duke shall know you better if I live to report you," said the Duke, grimly. Then he asked Escalus, whom he saw in the street, what he thought of his ducal master. Escalus, who imagined he was speaking to a friar, replied, "The Duke is a very temperate gentleman, who prefers to see another merry to being merry himself."

The Duke then proceeded to call on Mariana.

Isabella arrived immediately afterwards, and the Duke introduced the two girls to one another, both of whom thought he was a friar. They went into a chamber apart from him to discuss the saving of Claudio, and while they talked in low and earnest tones, the Duke looked out of the window and saw the broken sheds and flower-beds black with moss, which betrayed Mariana's indifference to her country dwelling. Some women would have beautified their garden: not she. She was for the town; she neglected the joys of the country. He was sure that Angelo would not make her unhappier.

"We are agreed, father," said Isabella, as she returned with Mariana.

So Angelo was deceived by the girl whom he had dismissed from his love, and put on her finger a ring he wore, in which was set a milky stone which flashed in the light with secret colors.

Hearing of her success, the Duke went next day to the prison prepared to learn that an order had arrived for Claudio's release. It had not, however, but a letter was handed to the Provost while he waited. His amazement was great when the Provost read aloud these words, "Whatsoever you may hear to the contrary, let Claudio be executed by four of the clock. Let me have his head sent me by five."

But the Duke said to the Provost, "You must show the Deputy another head," and he held out a letter and a signet. "Here," he said, "are the hand and seal of the Duke. He is to return, I tell you, and Angelo knows it not. Give Angelo another head."

The Provost thought, "This friar speaks with power. I know the Duke's signet and I know his hand."

249

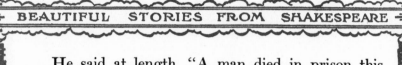

He said at length, "A man died in prison this morning, a pirate of the age of Claudio, with a beard of his color.   I will show his head."

The pirate's head was duly shown to Angelo, who was deceived by its resemblance to Claudio's.

The Duke's return was so popular that the citizens removed the city gates from their hinges to assist his entry into Vienna.   Angelo and Escalus duly presented themselves, and were profusely praised for their conduct of affairs in the Duke's absence.

It was, therefore, the more unpleasant for Angelo when Isabella, passionately angered by his treachery, knelt before the Duke, and cried for justice.

When her story was told, the Duke cried, "To prison with her for a slanderer of our right hand! But stay, who persuaded you to come here?"

"Friar Lodowick," said she.

"Who knows him?" inquired the Duke.

"I do, my lord," replied Lucio.   "I beat him because he spake against your Grace."

A friar called Peter here said, "Friar Lodowick is a holy man."

Isabella was removed by an officer, and Mariana came forward. She took off her veil, and said to Angelo, "This is the face you once swore was worth looking on."

Bravely he faced her as she put out her hand and said, "This is the hand which wears the ring you thought to give another."

"I know the woman," said Angelo. "Once there was talk of marriage between us, but I found her frivolous."

Mariana here burst out that they were affianced by the strongest vows. Angelo replied by asking the Duke to insist on the production of Friar Lodowick.

"He shall appear," promised the Duke, and bade Escalus examine the missing witness thoroughly while he was elsewhere.

Presently the Duke re-appeared in the character of Friar Lodowick, and accompanied by Isabella and the Provost. He was not so much examined as abused and threatened by Escalus. Lucio asked him to deny, if he dared, that he called the Duke a fool and a coward, and had had his nose pulled for his impudence.

251

"To prison with him!" shouted Escalus, but as hands were laid upon him, the Duke pulled off his friar's hood, and was a Duke before them all.

"Now," he said to Angelo, "if you have any impudence that can yet serve you, work it for all it's worth."

"Immediate sentence and death is all I beg," was the reply.

"Were you affianced to Mariana?" asked the Duke.

"I was," said Angelo.

"Then marry her instantly," said his master. "Marry them," he said to Friar Peter, "and return with them here."

"Come hither, Isabel," said the Duke, in tender tones. "Your friar is now your Prince, and grieves he was too late to save your brother;" but well the roguish Duke knew he had saved him.

"O pardon me," she cried, "that I employed my Sovereign in my trouble."

"You are pardoned," he said, gaily.

At that moment Angelo and his wife re-entered. "And now, Angelo," said the Duke, gravely, "we condemn thee to the block on which Claudio laid his head!"

"O my most gracious lord," cried Mariana, "mock me not!"

"You shall buy a better husband," said the Duke.

"Your Friar is Now Your Prince."

"O my dear lord," said she, "I crave no better man."

Isabella nobly added her prayer to Mariana's, but the Duke feigned inflexibility.

253

"Provost," he said, "how came it that Claudio was executed at an unusual hour?"

Afraid to confess the lie he had imposed upon Angelo, the Provost said, "I had a private message."

"You are discharged from your office," said the Duke. The Provost then departed. Angelo said, "I am sorry to have caused such sorrow. I prefer death to mercy." Soon there was a motion in the crowd. The Provost re-appeared with Claudio. Like a big child the Provost said, "I saved this man; he is like Claudio." The Duke was amused, and said to Isabella, "I pardon him because he is like your brother. He is like my brother, too, if you, dear Isabel, will be mine."

She was his with a smile, and the Duke forgave Angelo, and promoted the Provost.

Lucio he condemned to marry a stout woman with a bitter tongue.

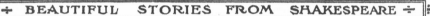

## TWO GENTLEMEN OF VERONA

ONLY one of them was really a gentleman, as you will discover later. Their names were Valentine and Proteus. They were friends, and lived at Verona, a town in northern Italy. Valentine was happy in his name because it was that of the patron saint of lovers; it is hard for a Valentine to be fickle or mean. Proteus was unhappy in his name, because it was that of a famous shape-changer, and therefore it encouraged him to be a lover at one time and a traitor at another.

One day, Valentine told his friend that he was going to Milan. "I'm not in love like you," said he, "and therefore I don't want to stay at home."

Proteus was in love with a beautiful yellow-haired girl called Julia, who was rich, and had no one to order her about. He was, however, sorry to part from Valentine, and he said, "If ever you are in

255

danger tell me, and I will pray for you." Valentine then went to Milan with a servant called Speed, and at Milan he fell in love with the Duke of Milan's daughter, Silvia.

When Proteus and Valentine parted Julia had not acknowledged that she loved Proteus. Indeed, she had actually torn up one of his letters in the presence of her maid, Lucetta. Lucetta, however, was no simpleton, for when she saw the pieces she said to herself, "All she wants is to be annoyed by another letter." Indeed, no sooner had Lucetta left her alone than Julia repented of her tearing, and placed between her dress and her heart the torn piece of paper on which Proteus had signed his name. So by tearing a letter written by Proteus she discovered that she loved him. Then, like a brave, sweet girl, she wrote to Proteus, "Be patient, and you shall marry me."

Delighted with these words Proteus walked about, flourishing Julia's letter and talking to himself.

"What have you got there?" asked his father, Antonio.

"A letter from Valentine," fibbed Proteus.

"Let me read it," said Antonio.

"There is no news," said deceitful Proteus; "he only says that he is very happy, and the Duke of Milan is kind to him, and that he wishes I were with him."

This fib had the effect of making Antonio think that his son should go to Milan and enjoy the favors in which Valentine basked. "You must go to-morrow," he decreed. Proteus was dismayed. "Give me time to get my outfit ready." He was met with the promise, "What you need shall be sent after you."

It grieved Julia to part from her lover before their engagement was two days' old. She gave him a ring, and said, "Keep this for my sake," and he gave her a ring, and they kissed like two who intend to be true till death. Then Proteus departed for Milan.

Meanwhile Valentine was amusing Silvia, whose grey eyes, laughing at him under auburn hair, had drowned him in love. One day she told him that she wanted to write a pretty letter to a gentleman whom she thought well of, but had no time: would

257

he write it? Very much did Valentine dislike writing that letter, but he did write it, and gave it to her coldly. "Take it back," she said; "you did it unwillingly."

VALENTINE WRITES A LETTER FOR SILVIA.

"Madam," he said, "it was difficult to write such a letter for you."

"Take it back," she commanded; "you did not write tenderly enough."

Valentine was left with the letter, and condemned

to write another; but his servant Speed saw that, in effect, the Lady Silvia had allowed Valentine to write for her a love-letter to Valentine's own self. "The joke," he said, "is as invisible as a weather-cock on a steeple." He meant that it was very plain; and he went on to say exactly what it was: "If master will write her love-letters, he must answer them."

On the arrival of Proteus, he was intro-duced by Valentine to Silvia and afterwards, when they were alone, Valentine asked Pro-teus how his love for Julia was prospering.

SILVIA READING THE LETTER.

"Why," said Proteus, "you used to get wearied when I spoke of her."

"Aye," confessed Valentine, "but it's different now. I can eat and drink all day with nothing but love on my plate and love in my cup."

"You idolize Silvia," said Proteus.

"She is divine," said Valentine.

"Come, come!" remonstrated Proteus.

"Well, if she's not divine," said Valentine, "she is the queen of all women on earth."

"Except Julia," said Proteus.

"Dear boy," said Valentine, "Julia is not excepted; but I will grant that she alone is worthy to bear my lady's train."

"Your bragging astounds me," said Proteus.

But he had seen Silvia, and he felt suddenly that the yellow-haired Julia was black in comparison. He became in thought a villain without delay, and said to himself what he had never said before—"I to myself am dearer than my friend."

It would have been convenient for Valentine if Proteus had changed, by the power of the god whose name he bore, the shape of his body at the evil moment when he despised Julia in admiring Silvia. But his body did not change; his smile was still affectionate, and Valentine confided to him the great secret that Silvia had now promised to run away with him. "In the pocket of this cloak," said Valentine, "I have a silken rope ladder, with hooks which will clasp the window-bar of her room."

Proteus knew the reason why Silvia and her lover were bent on flight. The Duke intended her to wed Sir Thurio, a gentlemanly noodle for whom she did not care a straw.

Proteus thought that if he could get rid of Valentine he might make Silvia fond of him, especially if the Duke insisted on her enduring Sir Thurio's tiresome chatter. He therefore went to the Duke, and said, "Duty before friendship! It grieves me to thwart my friend Valentine, but your Grace should know that he intends to-night to elope with your Grace's daughter." He begged the Duke not to tell Valentine the giver of this information, and the Duke assured him that his name would not be divulged.

Early that evening the Duke summoned Valentine, who came to him wearing a large cloak with a bulging pocket.

"You know," said the Duke, "my desire to marry my daughter to Sir Thurio?"

"I do," replied Valentine. "He is virtuous and

generous, as befits a man so honored in your Grace's thoughts."

"Nevertheless she dislikes him," said the Duke. "She is a peevish, proud, disobedient girl, and I should be sorry to leave her a penny. I intend, therefore, to marry again."

Valentine bowed.

"I hardly know how the young people of to-day make love," continued the Duke, "and I thought that you would be just the man to teach me how to win the lady of my choice."

"Jewels have been known to plead rather well," said Valentine.

"I have tried them," said the Duke.

"The habit of liking the giver may grow if your Grace gives her some more."

"The chief difficulty," pursued the Duke, "is this. The lady is promised to a young gentleman, and it is hard to have a word with her. She is, in fact, locked up."

"Then your Grace should propose an elopement," said Valentine. "Try a rope ladder."

"But how should I carry it?" asked the Duke.

"A rope ladder is light," said Valentine; "you can carry it in a cloak."

"Like yours?"

THE SERENADE.

"Yes, your Grace."

"Then yours will do. Kindly lend it to me."

263

Valentine had talked himself into a trap. He could not refuse to lend his cloak, and when the Duke had donned it, his Grace drew from the pocket a sealed missive addressed to Silvia. He coolly opened it, and read these words: "Silvia, you shall be free to-night."

"Indeed," he said, "and here's the rope ladder. Prettily contrived, but not perfectly. I give you, sir, a day to leave my dominions. If you are in Milan by this time to-morrow, you die."

Poor Valentine was saddened to the core. "Unless I look on Silvia in the day," he said, "there is no day for me to look upon."

Before he went he took farewell of Proteus, who proved a hypocrite of the first order. "Hope is a lover's staff," said Valentine's betrayer; "walk hence with that."

After leaving Milan, Valentine and his servant wandered into a forest near Mantua where the great poet Virgil lived. In the forest, however, the poets (if any) were brigands, who bade the travelers stand. They obeyed, and Valentine made so good an impression upon his captors that they offered him his life on condition that he became their captain.

"I accept," said Valentine, "provided you release my servant, and are not violent to women or the poor."

The reply was worthy of Virgil, and Valentine became a brigand chief.

We return now to Julia, who found Verona too dull to live in since Proteus had gone. She begged her maid Lucetta to devise a way by which she could see him. "Better wait for him to return," said Lucetta, and she talked so sensibly that Julia saw it was idle to hope that Lucetta would bear the blame of any rash and interesting adventure. Julia therefore said that she intended to go to Milan and dressed like a page.

"You must cut off your hair then," said Lucetta, who thought that at this announcement Julia would immediately abandon her scheme.

"I shall knot it up," was the disappointing rejoinder.

Lucetta then tried to make the scheme seem foolish to Julia, but Julia had made up her mind and was not to be put off by ridicule; and when her toilet was completed, she looked as comely a page as one could wish to see.

Julia assumed the male name Sebastian, and arrived in Milan in time to hear music being performed outside the Duke's palace.

"They are serenading the Lady Silvia," said a man to her.

Suddenly she heard a voice lifted in song, and she knew that voice. It was the voice of Proteus. But what was he singing?

> " Who is Silvia? what is she,
>     That all our swains commend her?
> Holy, fair, and wise is she;
>     The heaven such grace did lend her
> That she might admirèd be."

Julia tried not to hear the rest, but these two lines somehow thundered into her mind—

> " Then to Silvia let us sing;
>     She excels each mortal thing."

Then Proteus thought Silvia excelled Julia; and, since he sang so beautifully for all the world to hear, it seemed that he was not only false to Julia, but had forgotten her. Yet Julia still loved him. She even went to him, and asked to be his page, and Proteus engaged her.

One day, he handed to her the ring which she had given him, and said, "Sebastian, take that to the Lady Silvia, and say that I should like the picture of her she promised me."

Silvia had promised the picture, but she disliked Proteus. She was obliged to talk to him be-

ONE OF THE OUTLAWS.

cause he was high in the favor of her father, who thought he pleaded with her on behalf of Sir Thurio. Silvia had learned from Valentine that Proteus was pledged to a sweetheart in Verona; and when he said tender things to her, she felt that he was disloyal in friendship as well as love.

Julia bore the ring to Silvia, but Silvia said, "I will not wrong the woman who gave it him by wearing it."

"She thanks you," said Julia.

"You know her, then?" said Silvia, and Julia spoke so tenderly of herself that Silvia wished that Sebastian would marry Julia.

Silvia gave Julia her portrait for Proteus, who would have received it the worse for extra touches on the nose and eyes if Julia had not made up her mind that she was as pretty as Silvia.

Soon there was an uproar in the palace. Silvia had fled.

The Duke was certain that her intention was to join the exiled Valentine, and he was not wrong.

Without delay he started in pursuit, with Sir Thurio, Proteus, and some servants.

The members of the pursuing party got separated, and Proteus and Julia (in her page's dress) were by themselves when they saw Silvia, who had been taken prisoner by outlaws and was now being led to their Captain. Proteus rescued her, and then said, "I have saved you from death; give me one kind look."

"O misery, to be helped by you!" cried Silvia. "I would rather be a lion's breakfast."

Julia was silent, but cheerful. Proteus was so much annoyed with Silvia that he threatened her, and seized her by the waist.

"O heaven!" cried Silvia.

At that instant there was a noise of crackling branches. Valentine came crashing through the Mantuan forest to the rescue of his beloved. Julia feared he would slay Proteus, and hurried to help her false lover. But he struck no blow, he only said, "Proteus, I am sorry I must never trust you more."

Thereat Proteus felt his guilt, and fell on his knees, saying, "Forgive me! I grieve! I suffer!"

"Then you are my friend once more," said the generous Valentine. "If Silvia, that is lost to me, will look on you with favor, I promise that I will stand aside and bless you both."

These words were terrible to Julia, and she swooned. Valentine revived her, and said, "What was the matter, boy?"

"I remembered," fibbed Julia, "that I was charged to give a ring to the Lady Silvia, and that I did not."

"Well, give it to me," said Proteus.

She handed him a ring, but it was the ring that Proteus gave to Julia before he left Verona.

Proteus looked at her hand, and crimsoned to the roots of his hair.

"I changed my shape when you changed your mind," said she.

"But I love you again," said he.

Just then outlaws entered, bringing two prizes— the Duke and Sir Thurio.

"Forbear!" cried Valentine, sternly. "The Duke is sacred."

Sir Thurio exclaimed, "There's Silvia; she's mine!"

"Touch her, and you die!" said Valentine.

"I should be a fool to risk anything for her," said Sir Thurio.

"Then you are base," said the Duke. "Valentine, you are a brave man. Your banishment is over. I recall you. You may marry Silvia. You deserve her."

"I thank your Grace," said Valentine, deeply moved, "and yet must ask you one more boon."

"I grant it," said the Duke.

"Pardon these men, your Grace, and give them employment. They are better than their calling."

"I pardon them and you," said the Duke. "Their work henceforth shall be for wages."

"What think you of this page, your Grace?" asked Valentine, indicating Julia.

The Duke glanced at her, and said, "I think the boy has grace in him."

"More grace than boy, say I," laughed Valentine, and the only punishment which Proteus had to bear for his treacheries against love and friendship was the recital in his presence of the adventures of Julia-Sebastian of Verona.

HELENA AND BERTRAM.

## ALL'S WELL THAT ENDS WELL

IN the year thirteen hundred and something, the Countess of Rousillon was unhappy in her palace near the Pyrenees. She had lost her husband, and the King of France had summoned her son Bertram to Paris, hundreds of miles away.

Bertram was a pretty youth with curling hair,

finely arched eyebrows, and eyes as keen as a hawk's. He was as proud as ignorance could make him, and would lie with a face like truth itself to gain a selfish end. But a pretty youth is a pretty youth, and Helena was in love with him.

Helena was the daughter of a great doctor who had died in the service of the Count of Rousillon. Her sole fortune consisted in a few of her father's prescriptions.

When Bertram had gone, Helena's forlorn look was noticed by the Countess, who told her that she was exactly the same to her as her own child. Tears then gathered in Helena's eyes, for she felt that the Countess made Bertram seem like a brother whom she could never marry. The Countess guessed her secret forthwith, and Helena confessed that Bertram was to her as the sun is to the day.

She hoped, however, to win this sun by earning the gratitude of the King of France, who suffered from a lingering illness, which made him lame. The great doctors attached to the Court despaired of curing him, but Helena had confidence in a prescription which her father had used with success.

273

Taking an affectionate leave of the Countess, she went to Paris, and was allowed to see the King.

He was very polite, but it was plain he thought her a quack. "It would not become me," he said, "to apply to a simple maiden for the relief which all the learned doctors cannot give me."

"Heaven uses weak instruments sometimes," said Helena, and she declared that she would forfeit her life if she failed to make him well.

"And if you succeed?" questioned the King.

"Then I will ask your Majesty to give me for a husband the man whom I choose!"

So earnest a young lady could not be resisted for ever by a suffering king. Helena, therefore, became the King's doctor, and in two days the royal cripple could skip.

He summoned his courtiers, and they made a glittering throng in the throne room of his palace. Well might the country girl have been dazzled, and seen a dozen husbands worth dreaming of among the handsome young noblemen before her. But her eyes only wandered till they found Bertram. Then she went up to him, and said, "I dare not say I take you, but I am yours!" Raising her voice that the King might hear, she added, "This is the man!"

"Bertram," said the King, "take her; she's your wife!"

"My wife, my liege?" said Bertram. "I beg your Majesty to permit me to choose a wife."

"Do you know, Bertram, what she has done for your King?" asked the monarch, who had treated Bertram like a son.

"Yes, your Majesty," replied Bertram; "but why should I marry a girl who owes her breeding to my father's charity?"

"You disdain her for lacking a title, but I can give her a title," said the King; and as he looked at the sulky youth a thought came to him, and he added, "Strange that you think so much of blood when you could not distinguish your own from a beggar's if you saw them mixed together in a bowl."

"I cannot love her," asserted Bertram; and Helena said gently, "Urge him not, your Majesty. I am glad to have cured my King for my country's sake."

"My honor requires that scornful boy's obedience," said the King. "Bertram, make up your mind to this. You marry this lady, of whom you are so unworthy, or you learn how a king can hate. Your answer?"

Bertram bowed low and said, "Your Majesty has

HELENA AND THE KING.

ennobled the lady by your interest in her. I submit."

"Take her by the hand," said the King, "and tell her she is yours."

Bertram obeyed, and with little delay he was married to Helena.

276

Fear of the King, however, could not make him a lover. Ridicule helped to sour him. A base soldier named Parolles told him to his face that now he had a "kicky-wicky" his business was not to fight but to stay at home. "Kicky-wicky" was only a silly epithet for a wife, but it made Bertram feel he could not bear having a wife, and that he must go to the war in Italy, though the King had forbidden him.

Helena he ordered to take leave of the King and return to Rousillon, giving her letters for his mother and herself. He then rode off, bidding her a cold good-bye.

She opened the letter addressed to herself, and read, "When you can get the ring from my finger you can call me husband, but against that 'when' I write 'never.'"

Dry-eyed had Helena been when she entered the King's presence and said farewell, but he was uneasy on her account, and gave her a ring from his own finger, saying, "If you send this to me, I shall know you are in trouble, and help you."

She did not show him Bertram's letter to his wife; it would have made him wish to kill the truant

Count; but she went back to Rousillon and handed her mother-in-law the second letter. It was short and bitter. "I have run away," it said. "If the world be broad enough, I will be always far away from her."

"Cheer up," said the noble widow to the deserted wife. "I wash his name out of my blood, and you alone are my child."

The Dowager Countess, however, was still mother enough to Bertram to lay the blame of his conduct on Parolles, whom she called "a very tainted fellow."

Helena did not stay long at Rousillon. She clad herself as a pilgrim, and, leaving a letter for her mother-in-law, secretly set out for Florence.

On entering that city she inquired of a woman the way to the Pilgrims' House of Rest, but the woman begged "the holy pilgrim" to lodge with her.

Helena found that her hostess was a widow, who had a beautiful daughter named Diana.

When Diana heard that Helena came from France, she said, "A countryman of yours, Count

Rousillon, has done worthy service for Florence." But after a time, Diana had something to tell which was not at all worthy of Helena's husband. Bertram was making love to Diana. He did not hide the fact that he was married, but Diana heard from Parolles that his wife was not worth caring for.

The widow was anxious for Diana's sake, and Helena decided to inform her that she was the Countess Rousillon.

"He keeps asking Diana for a lock of her hair," said the widow.

Helena smiled mournfully, for her hair was as fine as Diana's and of the same color. Then an idea struck her, and she said, "Take this purse of gold for yourself. I will give Diana three thousand crowns if she will help me to carry out this plan. Let her promise to give a lock of her hair to my husband if he will give her the ring which he wears on his finger. It is an ancestral ring. Five Counts of Rousillon have worn it, yet he will yield it up for a lock of your daughter's hair. Let your daughter insist that he shall cut the lock of hair from her in a dark room, and agree in advance that she shall not speak a single word."

The widow listened attentively, with the purse of gold in her lap. She said at last, "I consent, if Diana is willing."

Diana was willing, and, strange to say, the prospect of cutting off a lock of hair from a silent girl in a dark room was so pleasing to Bertram that he handed Diana his ring, and was told when to follow her into the dark room. At the time appointed he came with a sharp knife, and felt a sweet face touch his as he cut off the lock of hair, and he left the room satisfied, like a man who is filled with renown, and on his finger was a ring which the girl in the dark room had given him.

The war was nearly over, but one of its concluding chapters taught Bertram that the soldier who had been impudent enough to call Helena his "kicky-wicky" was far less courageous than a wife. Parolles was such a boaster, and so fond of trimmings to his clothes, that the French officers played him a trick to discover what he was made of. He had lost his drum, and had said that he would regain it unless he was killed in the attempt. His attempt was a very poor one, and he was inventing the story of a heroic failure, when he was surrounded and disarmed.

READING BERTRAM'S LETTER.

"Portotartarossa," said a French lord.

"What horrible lingo is this?" thought Parolles, who had been blindfolded.

"He's calling for the tortures," said a French-

281

man, affecting to act as interpreter. "What will you say without 'em?"

"As much," replied Parolles, "as I could possibly say if you pinched me like a pasty." He was as good as his word. He told them how many there were in each regiment of the Florentine army, and he refreshed them with spicy anecdotes of the officers commanding it.

Bertram was present, and heard a letter read, in which Parolles told Diana that he was a fool.

"This is your devoted friend," said a French lord.

"He is a cat to me now," said Bertram, who detested our hearthrug pets.

Parolles was finally let go, but henceforth he felt like a sneak, and was not addicted to boasting.

We now return to France with Helena, who had spread a report of her death, which was conveyed to the Dowager Countess at Rousillon by Lafeu, a lord who wished to marry his daughter Magdalen to Bertram.

The King mourned for Helena, but he approved of the marriage proposed for Bertram, and paid a visit to Rousillon in order to see it accomplished.

"His great offense is dead," he said. "Let Bertram approach me."

Then Bertram, scarred in the cheek, knelt before his Sovereign, and said that if he had not loved Lafeu's daughter before he married Helena, he would have prized his wife, whom he now loved when it was too late.

"Love that is late offends the Great Sender," said the King. "Forget sweet Helena, and give a ring to Magdalen."

Bertram immediately gave a ring to Lafeu, who said indignantly, "It's Helena's!"

"It's not!" said Bertram.

Hereupon the King asked to look at the ring, and said, "This is the ring I gave to Helena, and bade her send to me if ever she needed help. So you had the cunning to get from her what could help her most."

Bertram denied again that the ring was Helena's, but even his mother said it was.

"You lie!" exclaimed the King. "Seize him, guards!" but even while they were seizing him, Bertram wondered how the ring, which he thought

Diana had given him, came to be so like Helena's.

A gentleman now entered, craving permission to deliver a petition to the King. It was a petition signed Diana Capilet, and it begged that the King

HELENA AND THE WIDOW.

would order Bertram to marry her whom he had deserted after winning her love.

"I'd sooner buy a son-in-law at a fair than take Bertram now," said Lafeu.

"Admit the petitioner," said the King.

Bertram found himself confronted by Diana and

284

her mother. He denied that Diana had any claim on him, and spoke of her as though her life was spent in the gutter. But she asked him what sort of gentlewoman it was to whom he gave, as to her he gave, the ring of his ancestors now missing from his finger?

Bertram was ready to sink into the earth, but fate had one crowning generosity reserved for him. Helena entered.

"Do I see reality?" asked the King.

"O pardon! pardon!" cried Bertram.

She held up his ancestral ring. "Now that I have this," said she, "will you love me, Bertram?"

"To the end of my life," cried he.

"My eyes smell onions," said Lafeu. Tears for Helena were twinkling in them.

The King praised Diana when he was fully informed by that not very shy young lady of the meaning of her conduct. For Helena's sake she had wished to expose Bertram's meanness, not only to the King, but to himself. His pride was now in shreds, and it is believed that he made a husband of some sort after all.

285

## PRONOUNCING VOCABULARY OF NAMES.

[*Key.*— a, e, i, o, u — as in *hat, bet, it, hot, hut;* ā, ē, ī, ō, ū — as in *ate, mete, mite, mote, mute;* ạ — as in *America, freeman, coward;* ĕ — as in *her, fern;* ŭ — as in *bŭrn, furl.*]

*Adriana* (ad-ri-ā'-nạ)
*Ægeon* (ē'-ge-on)
*Æmilia* (ē-mil'-i-ạ)
*Alcibiades* (al-si-bī'-ạ-dēz)
*Aliena* (ā-li-ē'-nạ)
*Angelo* (an'-je-lō)
*Antioch* (an'-ti-ok)
*Antiochus* (an-tī'-o-kus)
*Antipholus* (an-tif'-o-lus)
*Antonio* (an-tō'-ni-ō)
*Apemantus* (ap-e-man'-tus)
*Apollo* (ạ-pol'-ō)
*Ariel* (ā'ri-el)
*Arragon* (ar'-ạ-gon)
*Banquo* (ban'-kwō)
*Baptista* (bap-tis'-tạ)
*Bassanio* (bas-sā'-ni-ō)
*Beatrice* (bē'ạ-tris)
*Bellario* (bel-lā'-ri-ō)
*Bellarius* (bel-lā'-ri-us)
*Benedick* (ben'-e-dik)
*Benvolio* (ben-vō'-li-ō)
*Bertram* (bĕr'-tram)
*Bianca* (bē-an'-kạ)
*Borachio* (bō-rach'-i-ō)
*Brabantio* (brạ-ban'chō)
*Burgundy* (bŭr'-gun-di)
*Caliban* (kal'-i-ban)
*Camillo* (kạ-mil'-ō)

*Capulet* (kap'-ū-let)
*Cassio* (kas'-i-ō)
*Celia* (sē'-li-ạ)
*Centaur* (sen'-tawr)
*Cerimon* (sē'-ri-mon)
*Cesario* (se-sā'-ri-ō)
*Claudio* (klaw'-di-ō)
*Claudius* (klaw'-di-us)
*Cordelia* (kawr-dē'-li-ạ)
*Cornwall* (kawrn'-wawl)
*Cymbeline* (sim'-be-lēn)
*Demetrius* (de-mē'-tri-us)
*Desdemona* (des-de-mō'-nạ)
*Diana* (dī-an'-ạ)
*Dionyza* (dī-ō-nī'-zạ)
*Donalbain* (don'-al-bān)
*Doricles* (dor'-i-klēz)
*Dromio* (drō'-mi-ō)
*Duncan* (dung'-kạn)
*Emilia* (ē-mil'-i-ạ)
*Ephesus* (ef'e-sus)
*Escalus* (es'-kạ-lus)
*Ferdinand* (fĕr'-di-nand)
*Flaminius* (flạ-min'-i-us)
*Flavius* (flā'-vi-us)
*Fleance* (flē'-ans)
*Florizel* (flor'-i-zel)
*Ganymede* (gan'-i-mēd)
*Giulio* (jū'-li-ō)

286

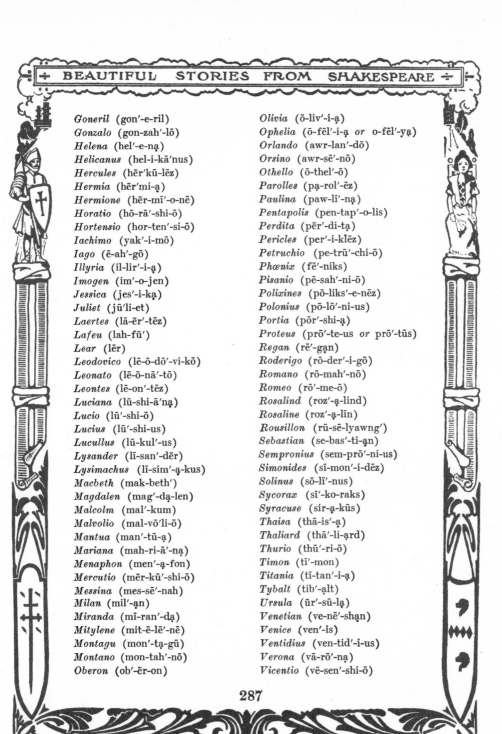

Goneril (gon'-e-ril)
Gonzalo (gon-zah'-lō)
Helena (hel'-e-nạ)
Helicanus (hel-i-kā'nus)
Hercules (hĕr'kū-lēz)
Hermia (hĕr'mi-ạ)
Hermione (hĕr-mī'-o-nē)
Horatio (hō-rā'-shi-ō)
Hortensio (hor-ten'-si-ō)
Iachimo (yak'-i-mō)
Iago (ē-ah'-gō)
Illyria (il-lir'-i-ạ)
Imogen (im'-o-jen)
Jessica (jes'-i-kạ)
Juliet (jū'li-et)
Laertes (lā-ēr'-tēz)
Lafeu (lah-fū')
Lear (lēr)
Leodovico (lē-ō-dō'-vi-kō)
Leonato (lē-ō-nā'-tō)
Leontes (lē-on'-tēz)
Luciana (lū-shi-ā'nạ)
Lucio (lū'-shi-ō)
Lucius (lū'-shi-us)
Lucullus (lū-kul'-us)
Lysander (lī-san'-dĕr)
Lysimachus (lī-sim'-ạ-kus)
Macbeth (mak-beth')
Magdalen (mag'-dạ-len)
Malcolm (mal'-kum)
Malvolio (mal-vō'li-ō)
Mantua (man'-tū-ạ)
Mariana (mah-ri-ā'-nạ)
Menaphon (men'-ạ-fon)
Mercutio (mĕr-kū'-shi-ō)
Messina (mes-sē'-nah)
Milan (mil'-ạn)
Miranda (mī-ran'-dạ)
Mitylene (mit-ē-lē'-nē)
Montagu (mon'-tạ-gū)
Montano (mon-tah'-nō)
Oberon (ob'-ĕr-on)

Olivia (ō-liv'-i-ạ)
Ophelia (ō-fēl'-i-ạ or o-fēl'-yạ)
Orlando (awr-lan'-dō)
Orsino (awr-sē'-nō)
Othello (ō-thel'-ō)
Parolles (pạ-rol'-ēz)
Paulina (paw-lī'-nạ)
Pentapolis (pen-tap'-o-lis)
Perdita (pĕr'-di-tạ)
Pericles (per'-i-klēz)
Petruchio (pe-trū'-chi-ō)
Phœnix (fē'-niks)
Pisanio (pē-sah'-ni-ō)
Polixines (pō-liks'-e-nēz)
Polonius (pō-lō'-ni-us)
Portia (pōr'-shi-ạ)
Proteus (prō'-te-us or prō'-tūs)
Regan (rē'-gạn)
Roderigo (rō-der'-i-gō)
Romano (rō-mah'-nō)
Romeo (rō'-me-ō)
Rosalind (roz'-ạ-lind)
Rosaline (roz'-ạ-līn)
Rousillon (rū-sē-lyawng')
Sebastian (se-bas'-ti-ạn)
Sempronius (sem-prō'-ni-us)
Simonides (sī-mon'-i-dēz)
Solinus (sō-lī'-nus)
Sycorax (sī'-ko-raks)
Syracuse (sir-ạ-kūs)
Thaisa (thā-is'-ạ)
Thaliard (thā'-li-ạrd)
Thurio (thū'-ri-ō)
Timon (tī'-mon)
Titania (tī-tan'-i-ạ)
Tybalt (tib'-ạlt)
Ursula (ŭr'-sū-lạ)
Venetian (ve-nē'-shạn)
Venice (ven'-is)
Ventidius (ven-tid'-i-us)
Verona (vă-rō'-nạ)
Vicentio (vē-sen'-shi-ō)

287

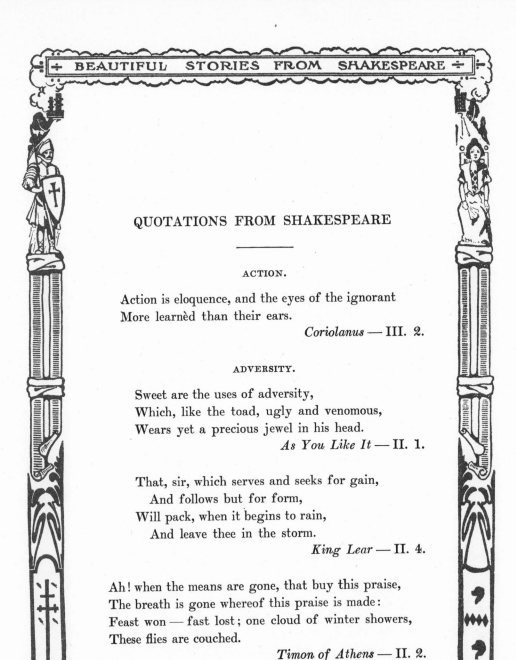

# QUOTATIONS FROM SHAKESPEARE

### ACTION.

Action is eloquence, and the eyes of the ignorant
More learnèd than their ears.

*Coriolanus* — III. 2.

### ADVERSITY.

Sweet are the uses of adversity,
Which, like the toad, ugly and venomous,
Wears yet a precious jewel in his head.

*As You Like It* — II. 1.

That, sir, which serves and seeks for gain,
And follows but for form,
Will pack, when it begins to rain,
And leave thee in the storm.

*King Lear* — II. 4.

Ah! when the means are gone, that buy this praise,
The breath is gone whereof this praise is made:
Feast won — fast lost; one cloud of winter showers,
These flies are couched.

*Timon of Athens* — II. 2.

### ADVICE TO A SON LEAVING HOME.

Give thy thoughts no tongue,
Nor any unproportioned thought his act
Be thou familiar, but by no means vulgar.
The friends thou hast, and their adoption tried
Grapple them to thy soul with hooks of steel;
But do not dull thy palm with entertainment
Of each new-hatched, unfledged comrade.   Beware
Of entrance to a quarrel: but, being in,
Bear it, that the opposer may beware of thee.
Give every man thine ear, but few thy voice:
Take each man's censure, but reserve thy judgment.
Costly thy habit as thy purse can buy,
But not expressed in fancy: rich, not gaudy:
For the apparel oft proclaims the man;
And they in France, of the best rank and station,
Are most select and generous, chief in that.
Neither a borrower, nor a lender be:
For loan oft loses both itself and friend;
And borrowing dulls the edge of husbandry.
This above all.— To thine ownself be true;
And it must follow, as the night the day,
Thou canst not then be false to any man.

*Hamlet* — I. 3.


### AGE.

My May of life
Is fallen into the sear, the yellow leaf:
And that which should accompany old age,
As honor, love, obedience, troops of friends,
I must not look to have; but, in their stead,

Curses not loud, but deep, mouth-honor, breath,
Which the poor heart would feign deny, but dare not.

*Macbeth* — V. 3.

### AMBITION.

Dreams, indeed, are ambition; for the very substance of the ambitious is merely the shadow of a dream. And I hold ambition of so airy and light a quality, that it is but a shadow's shadow.

*Hamlet* — II. 2.

I charge thee fling away ambition;
By that sin fell the angels, how can man then,
The image of his Maker, hope to win by 't?
Love thyself last; cherish those hearts that hate thee;
Corruption wins not more than honesty.
Still in thy right hand carry gentle peace,
To silence envious tongues.  Be just, and fear not!
Let all the ends, thou aim'st at, be thy country's,
Thy God's, and truth's.

*King Henry VIII.*—III. 2.

### ANGER.

Anger is like
A full-hot horse, who being allowed his way,
Self-mettle tires him.

*King Henry VIII.*— I. 1.

### ARROGANCE.

There are a sort of men, whose visages
Do cream and mantle like a standing pond,
And do a willful stillness entertain,

With purpose to be dressed in an opinion
Of wisdom, gravity, profound conceit,
As who should say, " I am Sir Oracle,
And when I ope my lips, let no dog bark ! "
O ! my Antonio, I do know of these
That therefore are reputed wise
For saying nothing, when, I am sure,
If they should speak, would almost dam those ears,
Which, hearing them, would call their brothers fools.

*The Merchant of Venice* — I. 1.

### AUTHORITY.

Thou hast seen a farmer's dog bark at a beggar?
And the creature run from the cur?
There thou might'st behold the great image of authority
    a dog's obeyed in office.

*King Lear* — IV. 6.

Could great men thunder
As Jove himself does, Jove would ne'er be quiet,
For every pelting, petty officer
Would use his heaven for thunder: nothing but thunder —
Merciful heaven !
Thou rather, with thy sharp and sulphurous bolt,
Splitt'st the unwedgeable and gnarled oak,
Than the soft myrtle ! — O, but man, proud man !
Drest in a little brief authority —
Most ignorant of what he's most assured,
His glassy essence,— like an angry ape,
Plays such fantastic tricks before high heaven,
As make the angels weep.

*Measure for Measure* — II. 2.

### BEAUTY.

The hand, that hath made you fair, hath made you good: the goodness, that is cheap in beauty, makes beauty brief in goodness; but grace, being the soul of your complexion, should keep the body of it ever fair.

*Measure for Measure* — III. 1.

### BLESSINGS UNDERVALUED.

It so falls out
That what we have we prize not to the worth,
Whiles we enjoy it; but being lacked and lost,
Why, then we rack the value; then we find
The virtue, that possession would not show us
Whiles it was ours.

*Much Ado About Nothing* — IV. 1.

### BRAGGARTS.

It will come to pass,
That every braggart shall be found an ass.
*All's Well that Ends Well* — IV. 3.

They that have the voice of lions, and the act of hares, are they not monsters?

*Troilus and Cressida* — III. 2.

### CALUMNY.

Be thou as chaste as ice, as pure as snow, thou shalt not escape calumny.

*Hamlet* — III. 1.

No might nor greatness in mortality
Can censure 'scape; back-wounding calumny
The whitest virtue strikes.  What king so strong,
Can tie the gall up in the slanderous tongue?
*Measure for Measure* — III. 2.


CEREMONY.

Ceremony
Was but devised at first, to set a gloss
On faint deeds, hollow welcomes.
Recanting goodness, sorry ere 'tis shown;
But where there is true friendship, there needs none.
*Timon of Athens* — I. 2.


COMFORT.

Men
Can counsel, and speak comfort to that grief
Which they themselves not feel; but tasting it,
Their counsel turns to passion, which before
Would give preceptial medicine to rage,
Fetter strong madness in a silken thread,
Charm ache with air, and agony with words:
No, no; 'tis all men's office to speak patience
To those that wring under the load of sorrow;
But no man's virtue, nor sufficiency,
To be so moral, when he shall endure
The like himself.
*Much Ado About Nothing* — V. 1.


Well, every one can master a grief, but he that has it.
*Idem* — II.

293

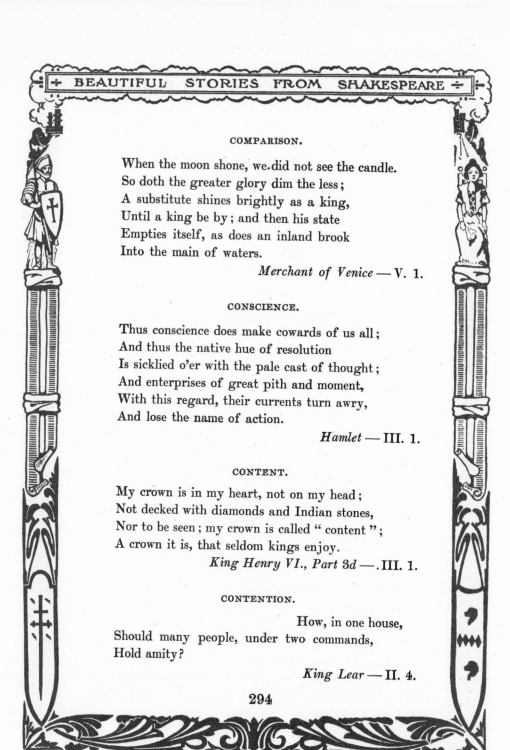

### COMPARISON.

When the moon shone, we.did not see the candle.
So doth the greater glory dim the less;
A substitute shines brightly as a king,
Until a king be by; and then his state
Empties itself, as does an inland brook
Into the main of waters.

*Merchant of Venice* — V. 1.

### CONSCIENCE.

Thus conscience does make cowards of us all;
And thus the native hue of resolution
Is sicklied o'er with the pale cast of thought;
And enterprises of great pith and moment,
With this regard, their currents turn awry,
And lose the name of action.

*Hamlet* — III. 1.

### CONTENT.

My crown is in my heart, not on my head;
Not decked with diamonds and Indian stones,
Nor to be seen; my crown is called " content ";
A crown it is, that seldom kings enjoy.

*King Henry VI., Part 3d* — .III. 1.

### CONTENTION.

How, in one house,
Should many people, under two commands,
Hold amity?

*King Lear* — II. 4.

When two authorities are set up,
Neither supreme, how soon confusion
May enter twixt the gap of both, and take
The one by the other.
                              *Coriolanus* — III. 1.

### CONTENTMENT.

'Tis better to be lowly born,
And range with humble livers in content,
Than to be perked up in a glistering grief,
And wear a golden sorrow.
                        *King Henry VIII.* — II. 3.

### COWARDS.

Cowards die many times before their deaths;
The valiant never taste of death but once.
                        *Julius Cæsar* — II. 2.

### CUSTOM.

That monster, custom, who all sense doth eat
Of habit's devil, is angel yet in this:
That to the use of actions fair and good
He likewise gives a frock, or livery,
That aptly is put on: Refrain to-night:
And that shall lend a kind of easiness
To the next abstinence: the next more easy:
For use almost can change the stamp of nature,
And either curb the devil, or throw him out
With wondrous potency.
                        *Hamlet* — III. 4.

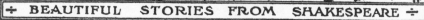

A custom
More honored in the breach, then the observance.

*Idem* — I. 4.

### DEATH.

Kings, and mightiest potentates, must die;
For that's the end of human misery.

*King Henry VI., Part 1st* — III. 2.

Of all the wonders that I yet have heard,
It seems to me most strange that men should fear;
Seeing that death, a necessary end,
Will come, when it will come.

*Julius Cæsar* — II. 2.

The dread of something after death,
Makes us rather bear those ills we have,
Than fly to others we know not of.

*Hamlet* — III. 1.

The sense of death is most in apprehension.

*Measure for Measure* — III. 1.

By medicine life may be prolonged, yet death
Will seize the doctor too.

*Cymbeline* — V. 5.

### DECEPTION.

The devil can cite Scripture for his purpose.
An evil soul, producing holy witness,
Is like a villain with a smiling cheek;

A goodly apple rotten at the heart;
O, what a goodly outside falsehood hath!

*Merchant of Venice* — I. 3.


### DEEDS.

Foul deeds will rise,
Though all the earth o'erwhelm them to men's eyes.

*Hamlet* — I. 2.


How oft the sight of means to do ill deeds,
Makes deeds ill done!

*King John* — IV. 2.


### DELAY.

That we would do,
We should do when we would; for this *would* changes,
And hath abatements and delays as many,
As there are tongues, are hands, are accidents;
And then this *should* is like a spendthrift sigh,
That hurts by easing.

*Hamlet* — IV. 7.


### DELUSION.

For love of grace,
Lay not that flattering unction to your soul;
It will but skin and film the ulcerous place;
Whiles rank corruption, mining all within,
Infects unseen.

*Hamlet* — III. 4.

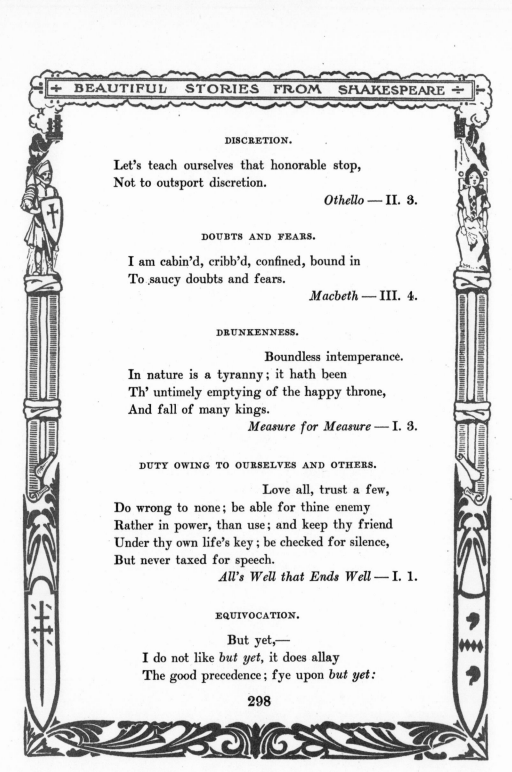

### DISCRETION.

Let's teach ourselves that honorable stop,
Not to outsport discretion.

*Othello* — II. 3.

### DOUBTS AND FEARS.

I am cabin'd, cribb'd, confined, bound in
To saucy doubts and fears.

*Macbeth* — III. 4.

### DRUNKENNESS.

Boundless intemperance.
In nature is a tyranny; it hath been
Th' untimely emptying of the happy throne,
And fall of many kings.

*Measure for Measure* — I. 3.

### DUTY OWING TO OURSELVES AND OTHERS.

Love all, trust a few,
Do wrong to none; be able for thine enemy
Rather in power, than use; and keep thy friend
Under thy own life's key; be checked for silence,
But never taxed for speech.

*All's Well that Ends Well* — I. 1.

### EQUIVOCATION.

But yet,—
I do not like *but yet*, it does allay
The good precedence; fye upon *but yet*:

*But yet* is as a gailer to bring forth
Some monstrous malefactor.
> *Antony and Cleopatra* — II. 5.

### EXCESS.

A surfeit of the sweetest things
The deepest loathing to the stomach brings.
> *Midsummer Night's Dream* — II. 3.

Every inordinate cup is unblessed, and the ingredient is
a devil.
> *Othello* — II. 3.

### FALSEHOOD.

Falsehood, cowardice, and poor descent,
Three things that women hold in hate.
> *Two Gentlemen of Verona* — III. 2.

### FEAR.

Fear frames disorder, and disorder wounds
Where it should guard.
> *King Henry VI., Part 2d* — V. 2.

Fear, and be slain; no worse can come, to fight:
And fight and die, is death destroying death;
Where fearing dying, pays death servile breath.
> *King Richard II.* — III. 2.

### FEASTS.

Small cheer, and great welcome, makes a merry feast.
> *Comedy of Errors* — III. 1.

### FILIAL INGRATITUDE.

Ingratitude! Thou marble-hearted fiend,
More hideous, when thou showest thee in a child,
Than the sea-monster.

*King Lear* — I. 4.

How sharper than a serpent's tooth it is
    To have a thankless child

*Idem* — I. 4.

### FORETHOUGHT.

        Determine on some course,
More than a wild exposure to each cause
That starts i' the way before thee.

*Coriolanus* — IV. 1.

### FORTITUDE.

            Yield not thy neck
To fortune's yoke, but let thy dauntless mind
Still ride in triumph over all mischance.

*King Henry VI., Part 3d* — III. 3.

### FORTUNE.

When fortune means to men most good,
She looks upon them with a threatening eye.

*King John* — III. 4.

### GREATNESS.

Farewell, a long farewell, to all my greatness!
This is the state of man: To-day he puts forth

The tender leaves of hope, to-morrow blossoms,
And bears his blushing honors thick upon him;
The third day, comes a frost, a killing frost;
And,— when he thinks, good easy man, full surely
His greatness is ripening,— nips his root,
And then he falls, as I do.

*King Henry VIII.*— III. 2.

Some are born great, some achieve greatness, and some
have greatness thrust upon them.

*Twelfth Night* — II. 5.

### HAPPINESS.

O, how bitter a thing it is to look into happiness through
another man's eyes.

*As You Like It* — V. 2.

### HONESTY.

An honest man is able to speak for himself, when a knave
is not.

*King Henry VI., Part 2d* — V. 1.

To be honest, as this world goes, is to be one man picked
out of ten thousand.

*Hamlet* — II. 2.

### HYPOCRISY.

Devils soonest tempt, resembling spirits of light.

*Love's Labor Lost* — IV. 3.

One may smile, and smile, and be a villain.

*Hamlet* — I. 5.

### INNOCENCE.

The trust I have is in mine innocence,
And therefore am I bold and resolute.

*Troilus and Cressida* — IV. 4.

### INSINUATIONS.

The *shrug,* the *hum,* or *ha;* these petty brands,
That calumny doth use;—

        For calumny will sear
Virtue itself:— these shrugs, these hums, and ha's,
When you have said, she's goodly, come between,
Ere you can say she's honest.

*Winter's Tale* — II. 1.

### JEALOUSY.

        Trifles, light as air,
Are, to the jealous, confirmations strong
As proofs of holy writ.

*Othello* — III. 3.

        O beware of jealousy:
It is the green-eyed monster, which does mock
The meat it feeds on.

*Idem.*

### JESTS.

A jest's prosperity lies in the ear of him that hears it.

*Love's Labor Lost* — V. 2.

He jests at scars, that never felt a wound.

*Romeo and Juliet* — II. 2.

### JUDGMENT.

Heaven is above all; there sits a Judge,
That no king can corrupt.

*King Henry VIII.*— III. 1.


### LIFE.

Life's but a walking shadow, a poor player,
That struts and frets his hour upon the stage,
And then is heard no more: it is a tale
Told by an idiot, full of sound and fury,
Signifying nothing.

*Macbeth* — V. 5.


We are such stuff
As dreams are made of, and our little life
Is rounded with a sleep.

*The Tempest* — IV. 1.


### LOVE.

A murd'rous guilt shows not itself more soon,
Than love that would seem hid: love's night is noon.

*Twelfth Night* — III. 2.


Sweet love, changing his property,
Turns to the sourest and most deadly hate.

*King Richard II.*— III. 2.


When love begins to sicken and decay,
It useth an enforced ceremony.

*Julius Cæsar* — II. 2.

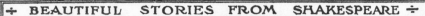

The course of true-love never did run smooth.
*Midsummer Night's Dream* — I. 1.

Love looks not with the eyes, but with the mind.
*Idem.*

She never told her love,—
But let concealment, like a worm i' th' bud,
Feed on her damask cheek: she pined in thought,
And, with a green and yellow melancholy,
She sat like Patience on a monument,
Smiling at grief.   Was not this love indeed?
*Twelfth Night* — II. 4.

But love is blind, and lovers cannot see
The pretty follies that themselves commit.
*The Merchant of Venice* — II. 6.

### MAN.

What a piece of work is man!  How noble in reason!
How infinite in faculties! in form, and moving, how express
and admirable! in action, how like an angel! in apprehension, how like a god! the beauty of the world! the paragon
of animals!

*Hamlet* — II. 2.

### MERCY.

The quality of mercy is not strained:
It droppeth, as the gentle rain from heaven,
Upon the place beneath: it is twice bless'd;
It blesses him that gives, and him that takes:

'Tis mightiest in the mightiest: it becomes
The throned monarch better than his crown:
His scepter shows the force of temporal power,
The attribute to awe and majesty,
Wherein doth sit the dread and fear of kings;
But mercy is above this sceptered sway;
It is enthroned in the hearts of kings;
It is an attribute to God himself;
And earthly power doth then show likest God's,
When mercy seasons justice.
                   Consider this,—
That, in the course of justice, none of us
Should see salvation: we do pray for mercy;
And that same prayer doth teach us all to render
The deeds of mercy.
             *Merchant of Venice* — IV 1.

### MERIT.

          Who shall go about
To cozen fortune, and be honorable
Without the stamp of merit! Let none presume
To wear an undeserved dignity.
            *Merchant of Venice* — II. 9.

### MODESTY.

It is the witness still of excellency,
To put a strange face on his own perfection.
            *Much Ado About Nothing* — II. 3.

### MORAL CONQUEST.

Brave conquerors! for so you are,
That war against your own affections,
And the huge army of the world's desires.

*Love's Labor's Lost* — I. 1.

### MURDER.

The great King of kings
Hath in the table of his law commanded,
That thou shalt do no murder.
Take heed; for he holds vengeance in his hand,
To hurl upon their heads that break his law.

*King Richard III.* — I. 4.

Blood, like sacrificing Abel's, cries,
Even from the tongueless caverns of the earth.

*King Richard II.* — I. 1.

### MUSIC.

The man that hath no music in himself,
Nor is not moved with concord of sweet sounds,
Is fit for treasons, stratagems, and spoils;
The motions of his spirit are dull as night,
And his affections dark as Erebus:
Let no such man be trusted.

*Merchant of Venice* — V. 1.

### NAMES.

What's in a name? that, which we call a rose,
By any other name would smell as sweet.

*Romeo and Juliet* — II. 2.

Good name, in man, and woman,
Is the immediate jewel of their souls:
Who steals my purse steals trash; 'tis something, nothing.
'Twas mine, 'tis his, and has been slave to thousands:
But he, that filches from me my good name,
Robs me of that, which not enriches him,
And makes me poor indeed.

*Othello* — III. 3.

### NATURE.

One touch of nature makes the whole world kin.
*Troilus and Cressida* — III. 3.

### NEWS, GOOD AND BAD.

Though it be honest, it is never good
To bring bad news.   Give to a gracious message
An host of tongues; but let ill tidings tell
Themselves, when they be felt.
*Antony and Cleopatra* — II. 5.

### OFFICE.

'Tis the curse of service;
Preferment goes by letter, and affection,
Not by the old gradation, where each second
Stood heir to the first.

*Othello* — I. 1.

### OPPORTUNITY.

Who seeks, and will not take when offered,
Shall never find it more.
*Antony and Cleopatra* — II. 7.

There is a tide in the affairs of men,
Which, taken at the flood, leads on to fortune;
Omitted, all the voyage of their life
Is bound in shallows, and in miseries:
And we must take the current when it serves,
Or lose our ventures.

*Julius Cæsar* — IV. 3.

### OPPRESSION.

Press not a falling man too far; 'tis virtue:
His faults lie open to the laws; let them,
Not you, correct them.

*King Henry VIII.*—III. 2.

### PAST AND FUTURE.

O thoughts of men accurst!
Past, and to come, seem best; things present, worst.

*King Henry IV., Part 2d* — I. 3.

### PATIENCE.

How poor are they, that have not patience! —
What wound did ever heal, but by degrees?

*Othello* — II. 3.

### PEACE.

A peace is of the nature of a conquest;
For then both parties nobly are subdued,
And neither party loser.

*King Henry IV., Part 2d* — IV. 2.

I will use the olive with my sword:
Make war breed peace; make peace stint war; make each
Prescribe to other, as each other's leech.

*Timon of Athens* — V. 5.

I know myself now; and I feel within me
A peace above all earthly dignities,
A still and quiet conscience.

*King Henry VIII.*—III. 2.

### PENITENCE.

Who by repentance is not satisfied,
Is nor of heaven, nor earth; for these are pleased;
By penitence the Eternal's wrath appeased.

*Two Gentlemen of Verona* — V. 4.

### PLAYERS.

All the world's a stage,
And all the men and women merely players:
They have their exits and their entrances;
And one man in his time plays many parts.

*As You Like It* — II. 7.

There be players, that I have seen play,— and heard
others praise, and that highly,— not to speak it profanely,
that, neither having the accent of Christians, nor the gait of
Christian, Pagan, nor man, have so strutted, and bellowed,
that I have thought some of nature's journeymen had made
men and not made them well, they imitated humanity so
abominably.

*Hamlet* — III. 2.

309

### POMP.

Why, what is pomp, rule, reign, but earth and dust?
And, live we how we can, yet die we must.
*King Henry V. Part 3d* — V. 2.

### PRECEPT AND PRACTICE.

If to do were as easy as to know what were good to do, chapels had been churches, and poor men's cottages princes' palaces.  It is a good divine that follows his own instructions: I can easier teach twenty what were good to be done, than be one of twenty to follow mine own teaching.  The brain may devise laws for the blood; but a hot temper leaps o'er a cold decree: such a hare is madness, the youth, to skip o'er the meshes of good counsel, the cripple.
*The Merchant of Venice* — I. 2.

### PRINCES AND TITLES.

Princes have but their titles for their glories,
An outward honor for an inward toil;
And, for unfelt imaginations,
They often feel a world of restless cares:
So that, between their titles, and low name,
There's nothing differs but the outward fame.
*King Richard III.* — I. 4.

### QUARRELS.

In a false quarrel these is no true valor.
*Much Ado About Nothing* — V. 1.

310

Thrice is he armed that hath his quarrel just;
And he but naked, though locked up in steel,
Whose conscience with injustice is corrupted.

*King Henry VI., Part 2d* — III. 2.

### RAGE.

Men in rage strike those that wish them best.

*Othello* — II. 3.

### REPENTANCE.

Men shall deal unadvisedly sometimes,
Which after-hours give leisure to repent.

*King Richard III.* — IV. 4.

### REPUTATION.

The purest treasure mortal times afford,
Is — spotless reputation; that away,
Men are but gilded loam, or painted clay.
A jewel in a ten-times-barred-up chest
Is — a bold spirit in a loyal breast.

*King Richard II.* — I. 1.

### RETRIBUTION.

The gods are just, and of our pleasant vices
Make instruments to scourge us.

*King Lear* — V. 3.

If these men have defeated the law, and outrun native punishment, though they can outstrip men, they have no wings to fly from God.

*King Henry V.* — IV. 1.

### SCARS.

A scar nobly got, or a noble scar, is a good livery of honor.
*All's Well that Ends Well* — IV. 5.

To such as boasting show their scars,
A mock is due.

*Troilus and Cressida* — IV. 5.

### SELF-CONQUEST.

Better conquest never can'st thou make,
Than arm thy constant and thy nobler parts
Against those giddy loose suggestions.

*King John* — III. 1.

### SELF-EXERTION.

Men at some time are masters of their fates;
    The fault is not in our stars,
But in ourselves.

*Julius Cæsar* — I. 2.

### SELF-RELIANCE.

Our remedies oft in ourselves do lie,
Which we ascribe to heaven: the fated sky
Gives us free scope; only, doth backward pull
Our slow designs, when we ourselves are dull.

*All's Well that Ends Well* — I. 1.

### SILENCE.

Out of this silence, yet I picked a welcome;
And in the modesty of fearful duty

I read as much, as from the rattling tongue
Of saucy and audacious eloquence.

*Midsummer Night's Dream* — V. 1.

The silence often of pure innocence
Persuades, when speaking fails.

*Winter's Tale* — II. 2.

Silence is the perfectest herald of joy: I were but little
happy, if I could say how much.

*Much Ado About Nothing* — II. 1.

### SLANDER.

Slander,
Whose edge is sharper than the sword; whose tongue
Outvenoms all the worms of Nile; whose breath
Rides on the posting winds, and doth belie
All corners of the world; kings, queens, and states,
Maids, matrons, nay, the secrets of the grave,
This viperous slander enters.

*Cymbeline* — III. 4.

### SLEEP.

The innocent sleep;
Sleep that knits up the raveled sleeve of care,
The death of each day's life, sore labor's bath,
Balm of hurt minds, great nature's second course,
Chief nourisher in life's feast.

*Macbeth* — II. 2.

**313**

### SUICIDE.

Against self-slaughter
There is a prohibition so divine,
That cravens my weak hand.

*Cymbeline* — III. 4.

### TEMPERANCE.

Though I look old, yet am I strong and lusty:
For in my youth I never did apply
Hot and rebellious liquors in my blood;
Nor did not with unbashful forehead woo
The means of weakness and debility:
Therefore my age is as a lusty winter,
Frosty, but kindly.

*As You Like It* — II. 3.

### THEORY AND PRACTICE.

There was never yet philosopher,
That could endure the tooth-ache patiently;
However, they have writ the style of the gods,
And made a pish at chance and sufferance.

*Much Ado About Nothing* — V. 1.

### TREACHERY.

Though those, that are betrayed,
Do feel the treason sharply, yet the traitor
Stands in worse case of woe.

*Cymbeline* — III. 4.

### VALOR.

The better part of valor is — discretion.
*King Henry IV., Part 1st* — V. 4.

When Valor preys on reason,
It eats the sword it fights with.
*Antony and Cleopatra* — III. 2.

What valor were it, when a cur doth grin
For one to thrust his hand between his teeth,
When he might spurn him with his foot away?
*King Henry VI., Part 1st* — I. 4.

### WAR.

Take care
How you awake the sleeping sword of war:
We charge you in the name of God, take heed.
*King Henry IV., Part 1st* — I. 2.

### WELCOME.

Welcome ever smiles,
And farewell goes out sighing.
*Troilus and Cressida* — III. 3.

### WINE.

Good wine is a good familiar creature, if it be well used.
*Othello* — II. 3.

O thou invisible spirit of wine, if thou hast no name to
be known by, let us call thee — devil! . . . O, that

men should put an enemy in their mouths, to steal away
their brains! that we should with joy, revel, pleasure, and
applause, transform ourselves into beasts!

*Othello* — II. 3.

### WOMAN.

A woman impudent and mannish grown
Is not more loathed than an effeminate man.

*Troilus and Cressida* — III. 3.

### WORDS.

Words without thoughts never to heaven go.

*Hamlet* — III. 3.

Few words shall fit the trespass best,
Where no excuse can give the fault amending.

*Troilus and Cressida* — III. 2.

### WORLDLY CARE.

You have too much respect upon the world:
They lose it, that do buy it with much care.

*Merchant of Venice* — I. 1.

### WORLDLY HONORS.

Not a man, for being simply man,
Hath any honor; but honor for those honors
That are without him, as place, riches, favor,
Prizes of accident as oft as merit;

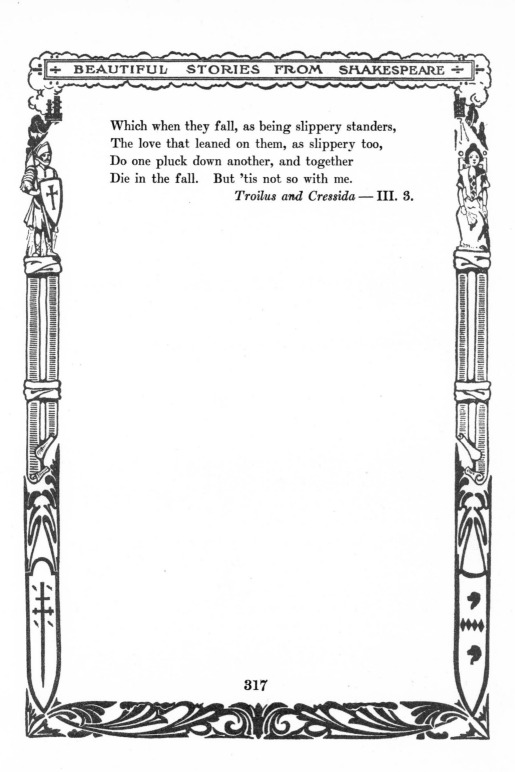

Which when they fall, as being slippery standers,
The love that leaned on them, as slippery too,
Do one pluck down another, and together
Die in the fall.   But 'tis not so with me.

*Troilus and Cressida* — III. 3.